COMING IN FOR A LANDING

TEN YEARS FLYING IN THE ISLANDS

BY

EMBRY RUCKER

AS TOLD TO HARRY ROTHGERBER

TRANSREAL BOOKS

Published December, 2017
Transreal Books, Los Gatos, California
www.transrealbooks.com

Paperback: ISBN 978-1-940948-27-0
Ebook: ISBN 978-1-940948-28-7

*Front cover photos are Embry and Noreen in South Caicos 1968,
and Embry flying a Cessna in 1968.*

*Back cover photo is a postcard of Grand Turk showing Embry,
Siofra, Noreen, and Embry III in 1973.*

For Noreen Smythe Rucker, my late wife,
Siofra and Embry, our children,
Joan M.W. Maclean, my wife,
and Rudy Rucker, my brother.

Contents

Preface

"The best mirror is an old friend." —*George Herbert*

In the 1980s, I noticed that some of my old friends and colleagues were dying—people I knew from the years that I spent flying in the West Indies. As I pondered death and mortality, my reflections about these friends made me realize how important that period of my life was to me, to Noreen and to the children. I concluded it was time for me to follow through on my plan to record some of the many stories about people, places and adventures that occurred during those years—before those memories were lost forever. I decided that it would be good for me to pass down the story of my life in the West Indies to my children, grandchildren and future generations. So in 1986, I wrote the first rough draft of my memories and stories.

Years later, I realized that I'd like to return to the Turks and Caicos Islands to visit the people and places that were such a significant part of my life for 10 years. So, after I stabilized the wood products company that I came to own, Noreen and I began returning to the Islands on a regular basis until 1998, when I sold the business.

On one of those trips, it was especially meaningful for me to pay a call to the plot of land that we had partial ownership rights to, near Conch Bar in Middle Caicos—to determine if it was really miserable like I had a feeling it was, or whether it was as beautiful and romantic as time and distance seemed to make it.

Then, around 2005, I decided it was important to record the stories of some of the aging folks in the Islands, since there really wasn't that much chronicled about the history of the Islands in the 1960s and '70s. So, I went to work, carried a tape recorder and interviewed more than 20 people throughout the Islands—mostly locals, plus some ex-pats living there. Later, I had a transcript made of all the interviews, which I gave, along with the original recordings, to the Turks and Caicos National Museum, located on Grand Turk. Some of those interviews will be quoted in these pages.

In 2015, through a mutual friend, I met Harry Rothgerber and learned that he could assist me in finalizing this story. While working with him, I was able to recall many more of my adventures in the Islands. With Harry's and my brother Rudy's assistance, these stories and recollections have been enlarged, revised and edited.

It is my hope that my children, Siofra and Embry III, will come to know me and their mother Noreen a little better because of these remembrances. Both born on Grand Turk, they may even wish to share these stories of the Islands with their children and with future generations of our family. I had great fun telling my stories to Harry, and I hope that you also enjoy them.

—Embry Cobb Rucker, Jr.
Louisville, Kentucky
September, 2017

Maps

The Caribbean

Caicos Islands

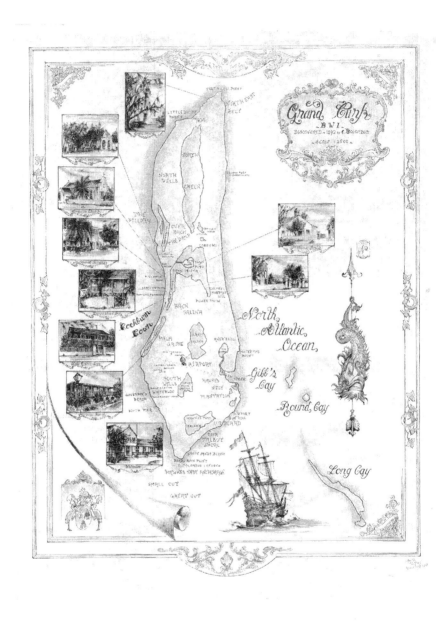

Grand Turk

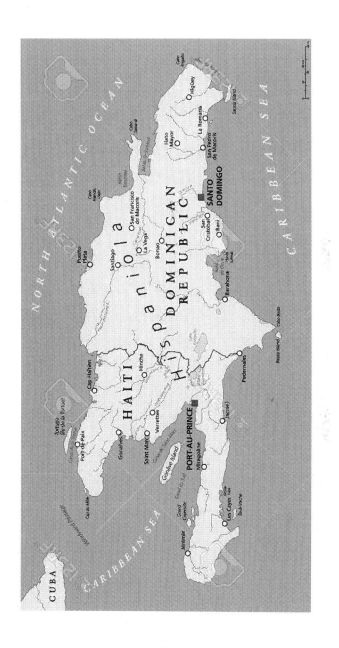

Haiti and Dominican Republic

Part I: Ten Years Flying in the Islands

Chapter 1: My Early Life

I was born in the Hahnemann University Hospital in Philadelphia, Pennsylvania on May 9, 1941, the son of Embry Cobb Rucker (1914-1994) and Marianne von Bitter Rucker (1916-1991). My full name is Embry Cobb Rucker Jr. My brother, Rudy Rucker, was born on March 22, 1946, three years after we moved to Louisville. His full name is Rudolf von Bitter Rucker.

Pop, as we called him, was born in New York City, a descendant of the Cobbs and Ruckers, both prominent Southern families, one of whom founded Ruckersville, Virginia in the 1600s. Why was he born up east? His father was originally in the insurance business in Athens, Georgia, but was transferred to New York. In fact, grandfather was a Vice-President of the Insurance Company of North America (INA), the oldest stock insurance company in the country, founded in 1792.

Mom was born in Hirschberg in the Silesian region of Germany, most of which is in modern-day Poland. Her parents were Wilhelm Herrmann Rudolf von Bitter (1880-1957), after whom my brother was named, and Louise Doraline Wilhemine "Lily" von Klenck (1888-1980). After growing up in Berlin, mother travelled to Philadelphia in 1937 to study art. This student exchange had been arranged by her oldest brother Franz, who had studied at nearby Swarthmore College.

I never realized that my mother spoke with a German accent until I was about 10 years old, and some other kid commented on it. She never lost that accent.

Although my father considered himself to be from Athens, Georgia, he grew up in the Philadelphia area— Bala-Cynwyd. He attended Virginia Military Institute (VMI), and graduated from there with a degree in civil engineering in 1936, after achieving some success as a varsity football player. In fact, we were always told that he later played center for the Wilmington (Delaware) Wheelers, a semi-pro team, for which he earned $5 a game. Father always said he went to VMI because his two brothers attended the Massachusetts Institute of Technology (MIT). His stock line was, "My two older brothers went to MIT—so I didn't." Actually, he decided to go there because an older classmate that he knew went there and liked it.

So, mother and father met in the Philadelphia area. My brother Rudy says that they were invited to a "suppressed desire" party, and that Pop showed up with a beer stein. In any event, after meeting and courting her— and proposing—Pop accompanied her back to Germany in 1938, and they married in Berlin on April 9, 1939, Easter Day. Due to the nature of the Nazi political regime at that time, father had to first prove to the authorities that he was of Aryan descent.

My parents returned to Philadelphia a few months later, and my father began working for Atlantic Steel Castings Company, the large iron and steel works business located in Chester, Pennsylvania, the town they lived in.

Anyway, Embry and Marianne Rucker eventually moved to Louisville in 1943 when he was hired by Tube Turns, Inc., which manufactured seamless forged pipefittings. In 1945, he was hired by B.F. Avery and Sons, Inc. as manager of the production-control department during an expansion of that company. Commonly called Avery Tractor Company, this business built agricultural machinery. As a result, when I was a child, my father would give me little toy tractors to play with.

Perhaps they chose to move here because my father's brother Tinsley already lived in Louisville and was plant manager for the Mengel Company, long-time woodworking company and manufacturer of furniture and other wooden items. Initially, my parents moved into a little house on River Road in the Harrods Creek area. Pop's other brother Cason eventually moved here from Ft. Thomas, Kentucky in 1947.

Some seven months after my birth, World War II began when the Japanese attacked Pearl Harbor on December 7, 1941, and the USA declared war on both Japan and Germany. Many young Americans rushed to recruiting stations to sign up for the struggle to come. Although he was trained as a cavalry officer at VMI, father wasn't allowed to enlist in our armed forces because he was married to a German national.

From the family history that I outline in Appendix One, it is evident that there are some prominent genealogical roots of my family; however, I still have many vivid memories about my own "good old days."

My childhood in Louisville was routine and uneventful; growing up in my family was very pleasant. Mother always had a snack ready for my brother and me when we returned home from school or play. I have a vivid memory of reading to my mother while sitting on a stone bench at our first house, and of mother being quite proud that I was mastering my Jack and Jill books, an early set of readers for youngsters. Although I look like my father in physical appearance, I inherited strong traits from both parents. I'm glad they were both smart.

My parents gave us a long leash. From 1944 to 1946, we lived in an historic farmhouse that we rented from the Dressel family on land across from Zachary Taylor National Cemetery. Known as the John Herr House, it was located at the end of a long driveway, the beginning of which was flanked by two large columns of brick and stone, right off Brownsboro Road. Currently located at

726 Waterford in the Wexford Place subdivision within Windy Hills, near the intersection of Brownsboro Road and Rudy Lane, it was one of the many extraordinary houses that were constructed by the Herr and Rudy families in that area. Built around 1795, it is now on the National Register of Historic Places.

My mother was always so nice and kind to Rudy and me. Remembering just one of her small kindnesses, I recall her always having a glass of milk and a piece of "honey bread"—bread slathered with honey—ready for us each day when we returned from school. She so loved her gardening, painting and pottery work; she was an artistic soul. That's why she came to Philadelphia in the first place—to study art.

For our next home, my parents bought two acres at 620 Rudy Lane in St. Matthews from Judge J. Paul Keith, Jr. and his wife Sarah, known by everyone as "Sally." The Keiths—at 612 Rudy Lane—became our next-door neighbors; they lived in the old George Herr home, the restoration of which was a lifelong project of Sally and her husband. This property was literally just a few hundred yards away from the John Herr House. Sally Keith eventually wrote the first grant for recognition of historic homes belonging to one family, in this case, the Herr family.

At the time father built the Rudy Lane house, he was associated with his friend Bill Straub, one of my Boy Scout leaders, in a business called the Dulaney Plywood Corporation, located at 1401 S. 12th Street. They built houses out of plywood—a new wood product at that time—which explains why the interior walls of the Rudy Lane house were all plywood. In fact, Dad thought that plywood was the greatest thing since sliced bread, as they say, especially when the manufacturers put a groove in it to make it look like paneling.

We did a lot of socializing with the Keiths, especially on Christmas Day. Some of my parents' other good friends were Dr. Philip Davidson, President of the University of Louisville from 1951 to 1968, and Dr. William C. Huffman, also from the University. My mother especially enjoyed gardening and was involved with various herb shows and gardening committees. Her obituary mentioned that she was "a potter, painter and creator of stained glass and a member of the Woman's Board at Norton Hospital."

The Keiths became good friends with everyone in our family; for many years, I remained connected to their son, attorney J. Paul Keith III, from whom I sought advice and assistance on several business dealings. Their oldest daughter, Sherry Keith (Jelsma), a few years older than me, became Secretary of the Kentucky Education, Arts and Humanities Cabinet, after serving on the Jefferson County School Board for eight years.

Another of my friends was David Hendon, who was later in my class at Louisville Country Day School—I haven't seen him for a long time. There was a photograph taken in 1951 showing David and me in a tree house with Frankie Thomas, Willie King, Bill Hewitt and Frankie Wilson. I don't recall any of those boys. Interestingly, two of the boys in the photo resided at Woodcock Hall, a facility for troubled boys. Located on Crestwood Avenue at Frankfort Avenue, this placement closed in 1955.

Near the Rudy Lane house there was a large field in which we would run and play, along with Nina and Muffin, our Springer spaniels. The church that we attended was St. Francis in the Fields Episcopal Church in Harrods Creek, about seven miles away, a straight drive out US 42. That church had been a constant in my life until recently when I started going to the Church of the Advent on Baxter Avenue at the foot of Broadway.

My father was very involved in our lives in a loving way, which led to a very good lifetime relationship between us. He was one of the adult leaders of my Boy Scout Troop #109, and he accompanied me on their field trips. It was also exciting when my father took us to old Parkway Field to see Johnny Unitas play for the University of Louisville football team during his four seasons as quarterback—1951 to 1954.

Eventually Pop left Avery Tractor Company for the Girdler Corporation, a gas and chemical company. He also achieved some distinction in the business department at the University of Louisville—Pop was an excellent college-level teacher. In 1949, while working full-time as the assistant works manager for Girdler, he headed up the first management institute for executive and staff management at the University's Law School. Coincidentally, in later years, I remember meeting Lynn Girdler, who was the daughter of the owner of that business—she was a renowned saddlebred horsewoman.

Occasionally, my father would take me on business trips with him when I was young; we travelled together to Chicago, Carolina, Tennessee and the Smokies. These journeys enabled me to view firsthand the operations of many manufacturing companies in the area. For me, even at that young age, the idea of making things was always interesting.

In addition, Rudy and I accompanied our mother on trips to Germany to visit our grandparents in the summers of 1950 and 1953.

Our first trip there was quite eventful. Mother and her two sons—ages 4 and 9—were taking a TWA Lockheed Super Constellation—a "Super Connie"—to Europe, with a refueling stop in Newfoundland, no doubt in Gander, a major refueling spot. Halfway to that destination, the plane lost one of its four engines! I can only imagine how frightened my mother—with two young children—must have been as the pilots turned the plane around and went back to New York City. The Super Connie can fly on three engines, but that situation had to be scary for her. To me, it was no big deal, because I was too young to grasp the import of that event. After safely arriving in New York, repairs were made, and we flew the same plane back to Newfoundland, then Shannon, Ireland, and on to Paris.

From Paris, we took a steam-locomotive train to Hanover, Germany. That is a memory that I'll not forget—it was hot, there was no air conditioning and the smoke from the engine was pouring in through the opened windows of the passenger cars. We were very uncomfortable, to say the least.

It appears that mother was not taking a chance on an airplane losing an engine when we returned to Germany in 1953, because we booked berths on an old freighter—my brother calls it a tramp steamer—named the *Karl Fisser*. Evidently, the owner of the shipping line had been a friend of my grandfather's, and that's why we booked passage on that vessel.

There were only two other passengers on the *Karl Fisser*, so Rudy and I had the run of the ship. Being young, curious kids, ages 7 & 12, we were shown everything by the amused crew members. We even had the opportunity to play chess with the captain on the bridge.

Strangely enough, young Rudy insisted on only eating pancakes during our voyage, and mother told the ship's cook to give him what he wanted. That explains why, upon arrival in Hamburg, the crew lined up and chanted, "Herr Prinz Pancake," as we passed by. In any event, we left the ship and again took a train to Hanover.

One of the places that I remember very vividly from these visits is Bad Pyrmont, a popular spa resort town in Lower Saxony. It impressed me because of the many injured German World War II veterans who were recuperating there; I don't recall ever seeing any injured soldiers in the States. Coincidentally, during the war, German prisoners were held in a camp right behind where the Quadrangle is located in Jeffersonville, not far from our father's future business—Champion Wood Products.

We had interesting visits with our German relatives. The zoo was only a 15 to 20-minute walk from where we were staying, and we went there regularly. There was a new elephant there, although the animal's black keeper appeared to be drawing as much attention as the elephant. There were few, if any, persons of color in that part of Germany at that time.

Our Uncle Conrad—mother's brother—had children our age, and we greatly enjoyed playing, swimming and going on picnics with our cousins during the six weeks that we spent with them.

The heightened sense of German discipline and responsibility struck me several times—literally. Once, a perfect stranger whacked me on the bottom when we were playing because I did something unruly. Another time, my grandfather Rudi gave me some candy and told me, "Don't show the other children," so they would not feel bad about not having candy themselves. Later, he happened to look out the window and see me do exactly what he cautioned me not to do. When I came back inside, I got a good whack and a lecture from him. These incidents were a real shock for a spoiled kid from the United States.

We would also spend time with Uncle Franz, another of mother's brothers, whose wife was Benedicta von Klencke; her family owned Schloss-Hämelschenburg— the Hämelschenburg Castle—a castle located near the town of Hameln, the site of the folk tale *The Pied Piper of Hamelin*. Sometimes we would have afternoon tea on top of the old castle walls which were 30 to 40 feet wide; inside, we would run down the long hallway flanked by many suits of armor on both sides.

Back in Louisville, my education was typical for the times. Early on, I developed an enjoyment of reading. Although I did not attend kindergarten, I performed pretty well at Greathouse Elementary (Grades 1-3), Lyndon Elementary (grades 4-5), Stivers Elementary (Grade 6), and then my final 6 years at the old Louisville Country Day School (LCD), located on Rock Creek Lane. The schools

I attended weren't very diverse; I can't say that there were ever any black students in class with me.

In the summer of 1958, I travelled with a group of friends and classmates to St. John's Camp at Delafield, Wisconsin; Mrs. Robert Becker, a very nice lady, accompanied us there. Jonathan Bingham, son of Mary and Barry Bingham, Sr., went with us—he and I were close friends. In fact, his father once took Jonathan and me to the downtown Armory to watch the professional wrestling matches.

Mr. Bingham, the newspaper owner and publisher, was a likeable guy who was known for sending handwritten notes to people to commemorate many occasions; Mrs. Bingham was also a nice person. As I said, Jonathan and I were good friends; also, we used to enjoy picking on his sister Eleanor, who was 4 or 5 years younger than us. Once, we found large caliber hunting rifles in the attic; they had been used by Jonathan's older brothers on an African safari. Needless to say, we also discovered sufficient ammo to fire the rifles at trees outside. Sadly, while I was away in the Army, Jonathan was electrocuted in an accident at his home.

My brother Rudy attended Louisville Country Day for 3 years and went to boarding school in Germany for the eighth grade. He then attended Catholic Country Day in the ninth grade. He was lucky enough to attend the 1958 World's Fair in Brussels with Uncle Conrad. Then Rudy transferred to St. Xavier High School, graduating in 1963. At St. X, he received many academic honors and awards, while being the school's "token Protestant."

Father served on the faculty of the University of Louisville School of Business for 15 years; he also worked as an independent engineering consultant for business, industry and hospitals, with offices in the Commonwealth Building downtown. In addition, he was working in the wood products industry, establishing a company in Jeffersonville called Champion Wood Products. However, at the age of 45, a new vocation called him—he began to pursue his desire to become an Episcopal minister. His yearning to seek this vocation may have started when he taught Sunday School at St. Francis.

In an unusual step, he didn't go to the seminary, but studied directly under Bishop C. Gresham Marmion for three years. While doing this, Pop became a deacon and served as lay reader at St. James Church in Shelbyville and Trinity Episcopal Church, which met at Zachary Taylor School on Westport Road. In fact, I remember going with him to Shelbyville and seeing the usher collecting the contributions not in a collection plate, but in his hat.

After passing all the training and education requirements of the Episcopal Board of Examining Chaplains, Pop was ordained at St. Francis in the Fields Church in Harrods Creek in 1959. My father's success was a big deal because he had not graduated from a traditional seminary. At the ordination, I was the crucifer, bearing the processional cross down the aisle.

After being ordained, he served as Associate under the Rector at St. Francis, Reverend Stephen R. Davenport, for two years or so. Father eagerly became involved in community and social work, always looking for ways to improve the lives of individuals. Later, in the 1970s, he served as an assistant in the office of Congressman Walter Fauntroy of the District of Columbia, and he was active in anti-Vietnam War activities, in civil rights and in the campaign for open housing. He once told me that he wanted to march against the war in Vietnam wearing a mitre, or bishop's headdress, on his head. Because I was in the Islands during the 1960s and '70s, I was out of touch with the cultural revolution and many protests and marches that were taking place in our country.

Various adventures happened to me in my teenage years—such as the bus trip to Jacksonville, Florida that I took by myself when I was 14 years old; the purpose was to visit Uncle Tinsley Rucker and his wife for a week.

My time with Uncle Tinsley went well, and he took me to catch the bus when it was time to return to Louisville. However, the bus driver told me that there were no more seats. Looking inside, I noticed some empty seats in the rear. The bus driver informed me, "That's the colored section." After thinking about it for a second, I replied, "I don't care, give me a ticket."

So, I rode to Louisville with a lot of very nice African-Americans who were on their way to Chicago, Detroit and other points north. Everyone was friendly, happy and very nice to me. Many had containers of fresh oranges and grapefruits that they were taking to relatives. In any event, I didn't mind being around black people—racism was never an issue in my family. It was a good trip home.

That was the same year that I went to Bloomfield, Kentucky and purchased a 1928 Ford Model A Roadster for 50 dollars. It was fun—but challenging—to restore it. When I turned 16 and could legally obtain a driver's license, I traded it for a sporty red 1931 Model A Roadster—that's the car that I drove when I passed my operator's license test. That was a very cool car; when a friend double-dated with me, he and his girl would sit in the rumble seat, an upholstered exterior seat that folded into what would have been the trunk. When I was 18, I got tired of it and sold it.

Between my sophomore and junior years at LCD, my father decided it would be best for me to depart Louisville for the summer, so I wouldn't be tempted to get into any trouble. My father was friends with Ed Gerber, who was the factory manager at Styline Industries, which owned a furniture manufacturing operation in Huntingburg, a small town in southwestern Indiana. So, Pop and I travelled up old Indiana Route 62 to check things out; and a little later, I drove my Model A up the same road and found myself residing in a rooming house, eating my nightly meals at the bus station and making 75 cents an hour—with a later raise to one dollar—for running a ripsaw and stacking lumber. What a life. Was I ever glad to return to school!

All joking aside, my parents were generally very kind and patient with me. Of course, a certain amount of conflict inevitably takes place between parents and their adolescent sons with raging hormones. When my own son was a teenager, my father once told him, "Embry, we get along so well because we have a common enemy." Of course, the enemy was Me. That was a creative and insightful way to describe generational conflicts that occur over the course of time.

It was probably beneficial to our overall physical health and well-being that participation in athletics at LCD was compulsory for every student; practices and events took place from 3:00 to 5:00 every afternoon. We were split into two competing groups—the Blues and the Grays. Civil War, anyone?

Among the organizations in which I was active were: Chevalier Literary Society, a Louisville social and writing club that originated at Male High School—my brother was later a member; Youth Speaks–I still see my classmates Jay Norman and Lewis Seiler every now and then; *The Descrier*, our literary magazine—classmate Jim Van Cleave, the smartest guy I ever met, has been living on a commune in Colorado about 50 years; the Dramatic Club—I portrayed a camp guard in our production of *Stalag 17*, based on the Academy Award-winning movie about a POW camp in World War II Germany; and, the Wrestling team—Becoming pretty decent, I had fun and strove to be "leather-tough and panther-quick." Since there were only two schools which then wrestled for the state championship—LCD and Kentucky School for the Blind—I became state champion at 147-157 pounds. Not being into basketball, I played on the varsity Football team for two years, the Soccer team one year and the Tennis team for three years.

Although LCD was not a particularly known for its academic excellence, it was highly successful at getting graduates into the colleges they desired. In general, I liked high school, and LCD was alright. There were only 30 in my class, and we all knew each other. Most all of us later became successful in some field, such as Larry Crutcher, a top executive with Time, Inc.; Jay Norman, who owned a publishing company; Robert Lisle Baker, a Suffolk University law school professor and elected official, with whom I just had lunch in February 2017; and, Ken Hirsch, president of Paramount Foods, Inc., just to mention several.

As a Louisville Country Day School junior in March 1959, my parents allowed me to take a spring break trip to Florida—three carloads of my friends and I went to the sunny east coast beaches for a week. It was a week of sun and fun in Florida and my first time in the North Miami Beach area. Corwin "Corky" Short and I stayed with David Owen's grandparents, Mr. and Mrs. C. K. Reynolds.

Well, Corky, David and I looked for trouble there but couldn't find a lot of it. David's grandfather rented a car for us, and we put a lot of miles on it going up to Fort Lauderdale and Delray Beach, about 40 miles away. In those days, you paid for rental cars by the number of miles that you drove. David and I were both big car enthusiasts, and we got the bright idea that if you put the car up in blocks and ran it in reverse, you could erase mileage from its total. Nope. Didn't work.

In later years, Corky and his wife used to own and operate The Kite Store in the old downtown Louisville Galleria; he died not long ago. David lives in Richmond, Virginia; I saw him at our last LCD reunion.

Graduating from LCD, I then attended Kenyon College, a private liberal arts college in Gambier, Ohio, about 50 miles northeast of Columbus. Kenyon was the first of several schools that I attended in pursuit of my eventual college degree.

In 1961, I spent my spring vacation with my parents in Louisville, because mother's mother had come over from Hanover, Germany for a three-month visit. However, I was so self-absorbed at that time that I neglected to ask her anything substantial about her life in Germany. Of course, she had only lived through both World Wars, having been bombed out in the second one. One of my regrets was not knowing her better. One fascinating thing that I did learn was that she was famous for her speedy troika-driving. A troika is a traditional Russian harness driving combination, with three horses pulling a sleigh.

Time marches on, and after two so-so years at Kenyon College, my father introduced me to the Army recruiter; in 1962, I signed up for three years and began doing my own marching.

The following year, while I was away protecting our country, Pop left St. Francis to start the mission of St. Aidan's in Alexandria, Virginia. This was about the same time that my brother enrolled in and began his first year at Swarthmore College in Pennsylvania, which Uncle Franz had attended. In the same time frame, my parents sold the house and left Louisville.

In 1967, under Pop's watch, St. Aiden's became an actual parish. Then, in early 1969, he assumed the duties as vicar of an Episcopal congregation in Reston, Virginia. Dad always said, "You don't need new church buildings—there are always buildings you can use." During the same interval, he was one of eight ministers nominated for bishop of the Episcopal Diocese of Virginia. He wasn't chosen. But he was happy, and I can picture him just standing on the dock at Lake Anne, surveying the flora, fauna and man-made surroundings.

Reston, founded in 1964, was in the Northern Virginia-Washington area. It was unique in that it was one of the country's first planned communities, a site which the founder—Robert E. Simon, Jr.—wanted to be more than a *place* to live; he wanted Reston to be a *way* to live. Simon's background was unique. After graduating from Harvard, he took over the family real estate business. In 1961, with the proceeds from the sale of New York

City's famous Carnegie Hall, a family property, Simon purchased 6,750 acres of land in Fairfax County, Virginia and developed a master plan for the new town of Reston. The town's name was derived from Simon's initials and the word "town."

Simon was quite a visionary—his new town concept emphasized an improved quality of life for the individual and provided a community where people could live, work, and play without driving long distances. Be that as it may, although Reston was OK, I didn't like the new town concept a lot when I stayed there. Now, many years later, I wouldn't mind living there or in a similar community.

Father could afford the ministry only because of the financial success of his Champion Wood Products business, which he still owned in Jeffersonville. One of his employees was assigned to operate it while Pop was in Virginia; my father would fly back once a month to check the books and see how things were going. He greatly enjoyed living in Reston and had no desire to return to Louisville. More about that later.

Back to me again: Having volunteered to serve in Uncle Sam's Army, I went through a series of tests to determine my proficiencies. The results showed that I had good language aptitude—that would have certainly surprised my Latin and French teachers in high school. It certainly surprised me.

As a result, I was sent to the Army Language School in Monterey, California. Now, this was early in the Vietnam War, when things were just starting to heat up. On our first day in class, one of our instructors addressed us. He told us that we could put forth effort, study and learn foreign language, or we could go across the street to Fort Ord for training in a combat infantry outfit and get shot at in Vietnam. "The choice is yours," he concluded. An easy one to make for me.

Six months later, having successfully completed Army Language School, my military occupation specialty became

Interpreter/Translator. I was sent to Germany—of all places—for two years. Lucky me.

At that point, my fluency in German was superior. Under operational control of the National Security Agency, I was assigned to the border, where I spent most of my time monitoring East German radio transmissions of various types. Thankfully, I was also able to visit my mother's German relatives while I was in service to Uncle Sam. All in all, an excellent assignment.

Chapter 2: Learning to Fly

"Your life will fly by, so make sure you're the pilot."
—*Rob Liano*

Well, that brings my story up to 1965, when I was honorably discharged from the Army after fulfilling my three-year commitment. For a while after leaving the service, I travelled around Germany, seeing more of that country's sights. By the time I returned to the States, my parents had moved to Virginia following my father's full-time commitment to the Episcopal ministry.

Living in my family's new home in Alexandria, I enrolled in a night school program at the nearby University of Maryland, where I majored in Economics. But in one of those key life moments, I decided to attend flight school training during the day in Manassas, Virginia. Why? A friend of my father was a pilot for United Airlines, and he said that their pilots only worked about 80 hours a month and got paid handsomely. That sounded like a pretty good deal to me, so I decided to give it a shot. By the way, I eventually concluded my college odyssey by successfully graduating from the University of Louisville—some 20 years later.

Every now and then, I would return to Louisville for a brief visit. For example, Steve Davenport, a good friend through high school, was married; I returned to be an usher in the wedding. Steve and I were close in those days, but I don't see him much anymore, as the years have intervened.

After a year and a half, while still attending both the University and flight school, I had earned my commercial pilot's license, instrument rating and multi-engine rating. Also, I had become friendly with a fellow named Gray Lang, Jr. who was the Legislative Assistant to Rogers C. B. Morton, the U.S. Congressman representing Maryland's Eastern Shore district.

Rogers was a member of the Morton family that was prominent in Kentucky business and politics; his brother Thruston served in the U.S. Senate from 1957 to 1968.

Anyway, Gray Lang and I got to be good friends, and we frequently talked about flying. On one occasion in 1966, Gray told me that he and Rogers were going to trade in their Cessna 182 Skylane on a twin-engine Aero Commander 560A. The Skylane, a four-seat, single-engine plane introduced in 1956, was the second-most popular Cessna, right after the 172. The Aero Commander was a high-wing, piston-engine, civil utility aircraft that could carry seven people. It had more power and higher performance than its predecessors. There were only 99 of this model built. They knew that I had a multi-engine rating, so they asked if I would fly with them on a trip down to the Bahamas—in order to instruct them on how to handle their new aircraft. Since I desperately wanted a flying job at that time, I replied, "Sure, no sweat," even though I had never flown anything like that before.

They took me at my word, and shortly after that we all flew in the Cessna to Kip DuPont's place, Summit Aviation in Delaware, to take delivery of the Aero Commander. It was through Rog that I met Richard C. DuPont, Jr., better known as "Kip," who had learned to fly at age 16 and was founder of Summit Aviation in Middletown, Delaware. A member of the prominent DuPont family, Kip's father was a renowned aviation and glider pioneer.

I hoped that somebody was going to check me out before I actually flew anything that looked as complex as the Aero Commander.

When we arrived, we met an airplane dealer and flight instructor named Holliday from Richmond, Virginia who looked to be in his 60s or 70s, and who was making delivery of the aircraft. Well, I'll tell you how old he was—his pilot's license was signed by Orville Wright, the airplane inventor brother who died in 1948! He had been around awhile. The old-timer asked me, "Got much time in the Aero Commander, boy?" To which I replied, "No, sir." Then he questioned, "You got much multi-engine time?" And I answered, "No, sir." Then he got a little quieter and asked, "How much multi-engine time do you have?" My response, in a whisper, was "About seven hours." Whereupon he sidled over to Rog and stated, "Uh, Congressman Morton, I think what I'll do is, I'll go along with you on this first trip down to the Bahamas and just make sure the aircraft runs alright, and make sure your young fellow here knows how to fly it and make sure we got no problems." Hearing that, I breathed an enormous sigh of relief because since I had a look at the Commander, I realized that this airplane was a little more complicated than I thought.

So, I lucked out, and Mr. Holliday and I had a great flight down there. He was a splendid instructor. For example: In the Aero Commander, proper procedure is for you to always put the gear handle down when you want the landing wheels down, and then you lock it down. But, with that on my mind, I kept making a mistake. When we'd go wheels up, I'd lock those up, too. Holliday had directed me twice never to do that, telling me it was a mistake locking them up, that I may try to land with the wheels up if I kept doing that. Finally, after the third time I mistakenly did it, he whacked me on the arm really hard—I started to remember after that!

By the way, I read an article that appeared in the *Lexington Herald-Leader* in 2012 which indicated that Gray Lang still loved flying—he and his son Graeme, a pilot for the Kentucky Department of Aviation, were planning to fly a twin-engine Beech Baron from Georgetown, Kentucky all the way to England and back.

Back to my story: By the time that we arrived in Nassau, the capital of the Bahamas, in one piece, and then, after refueling, flew on to Georgetown Exuma, I felt that I knew the airplane fairly well. We—Rog and Ann Morton, Gray and Missy Lang and I—all had a great time down there. Rog Morton was a terrific guy.

While there, I met some partners of Roger's in a venture in the Turks and Caicos Islands. The official name of this corporate association was Provident, Ltd. The seven partners were: Fritz Ludington, the fairly wealthy owner of the Two Turtles Inn at Georgetown and an enterprising investor and entrepreneur; Fritz's mother, Mrs. Barber, from Birmingham, Alabama—although she didn't travel to the Islands very often; Teddy Roosevelt III, former Naval Aviator and grandson of former President Theodore Roosevelt—he was a really nice fellow whose wife Ann was a Louisvillian and perhaps related to the Mortons; Kip DuPont and Rogers Morton, both of whom I mentioned earlier; Peter Thompson, Rog's campaign manager from the Eastern Shore; and lastly, Tommy Coleman, whom I will tell you about in more detail later. The group asked if I was interested in assisting them in a new project that they had in the Turks and Caicos Islands, specifically on the island of Providenciales—commonly known as "Blue Hills" by the locals—as their *bookkeeper*!

Now, Provident, Ltd. still operates to this very day, with my friend Bengt Söderqvist, one of their original employees, as the main contact in both Providenciales—known as "Provo" to many—and Wellington, Florida, near West Palm Beach. I'm not exactly sure who owns it, but it now specializes in the development of commercial and residential properties. All the original partners have passed away.

Although I knew nothing at all about keeping books, I strongly wanted that job because I had developed a real liking for the Islands. So I answered, "Sure, I'd be glad to, just let me go back to Virginia to collect my belongings, and I'll return in a couple of weeks." They replied affirmatively, and I had a new job!

Now, this offer, acceptance and new plan took place over the Christmas holidays, and Rog, being the great guy he was, wanted me to have some more flying time in the airplane. He suggested that I just take the Commander on my trip back to Virginia to spend some time with my family for Christmas; then, on the way back to the Islands, I could pick up some steaks from a friend of his in Easton, Maryland. Transporting steaks—what an amazing reason to fly an Aero Commander a total of 1500 miles!

When I completed the solo trip back to Virginia, I began to feel very confident in my ability to handle the airplane. After visiting my family in Virginia and picking up the steaks in Easton, I returned to the Islands.

In early 1967, I flew back to Virginia again, this time with Rog, the Thompsons and a young girl I'd met in Georgetown who was doing some babysitting for the Langs. Her Italian-American uncle was an important official in the Hod Carriers Union, officially known as the Laborers International Union of North America—I noticed this when I dropped her off in DC at his office building. Suffice it to say that my parents were somewhat less than enthused to meet her.

Well, when I arrived home in Virginia and announced to my parents that I had a job as a bookkeeper, my business-school-professor father pointed out to me that it might be a good idea to learn something about the general concept of bookkeeping. As a result, I went straight out and bought a book titled, *How to Be a Bookkeeper in Ten Days or Less*, or something like that. After studying it, I came to a mental understanding about the meaning of debits and credits and balance sheets and that sort of thing. I figured that if all I had to do was keep track of the checkbook, then I could handle that assignment. More about my misconception of that that job task later.

So, having obtained the job I wanted, I got my MG Midget ready to roll—my father would tell you that was about my tenth car by then—since before that I'd...oh, well, never mind. I intended to mention something about the Jaguar sedan, but I had forgotten that the Jag came later—the Porsche 1600 actually came before the MG. At least Rudy appeared to be impressed with the number of vehicles that I bought and sold. In any event, off to Florida I drove in a fast set of wheels.

Chapter 3: Tommy, Fritz and The Seven Dwarfs

"Crazy loves company." —*Marissa Meyer*

Arriving in the Sunshine State after driving down from Alexandria, Virginia, I met Fritz Ludington at the Delray Beach Yacht Club. There, for the first time, I saw the ship called the *Seven Dwarfs*, a 65-foot freight boat officially operating out of Pompano Beach, where Fritz maintained a residence.

Later, I found out that the *Seven Dwarfs* was named for the seven partners in the Providenciales venture in which I was involved: Fritz, Teddy, Rog and the others. Here's how the conversation went between Fritz and me:

Fritz: "Well, the first thing is, I want you to get on the boat and you be the navigator."

Me: "I don't know anything about boats, all I've been on are little outboards on the Ohio River."

Fritz: "Well, you know how to fly, don't you?"

Me: "Yes."

Fritz: "Well, you know how to navigate while you fly, don't you?"

Me: "Yes."

Fritz: "Same thing—no sweat—just slower."

Then, walking off, he pointed to a man standing nearby and said, "Oh, by the way, that's Tommy, he'll be the Captain. You'll be working with him." I just stood there, not knowing what to do, when Tommy Coleman called out, "Come over here, boy." Walking down into the hold of this boat, he continued, "Come on down here and give me a hand with this cement." The whole situation was really bizarre, but all of a sudden, I was down in the hold of a small freighter loading cement—94-pound bags of cement. The cement just kept coming, and Tommy and I just kept stacking it. Finally, after what seemed like hours, Tommy looked at me sideways, kind of grinned and asked, "How do you like being a bookkeeper?"

Ha! At that moment, I really didn't know how to respond to Tommy's question. I was convinced that I'd gotten hooked up with a bunch of lunatics, which turned out to be more or less true—but they all turned out to be great guys. I also found out that Tommy Coleman, from Boggy Creek, Florida, was one of the seven partners in this venture.

By the way, I had given the girl I mentioned before— the Lang's babysitter—a ride down to Florida from Virginia, so she was temporarily staying at Fritz's with me and Tommy and the others. She didn't really know what she was doing there with all of us, but when she took one look at the *Seven Dwarfs*, she evidently decided she didn't want to be any part of that, whatever that was. So off she went.

Eventually, Tommy and I succeeded in loading the boat, and the two of us cast off from the Delray Beach Yacht Club.

Our relationship with the Yacht Club was a story in itself. It really was a very nice place, known now as The Yacht Club at Delray Beach. Why they let us in there with that filthy old cargo boat, I have no idea. Tommy would drive them insane when he would steer in towards the dock and loudly shout at me, "Embry, I'm going to hit her with the pointy end—you jump off and grab a rope and then I'll see if I can get the blunt end in." Generally, this activity very quickly drew a crowd of curious yachtsmen dressed in their all-whites with little gold bullion caps and all the decorative trimmings. Of course, the two of us were usually just plain filthy when we returned from one of these trips.

I'd shout, "Okay, hit her with the pointy end and I'll jump off." Sure enough, Tommy would smash the dock with the "pointy end," I'd jump off with a rope and the "blunt end" would come crashing in on the other end of the dock. Then I would jump back on, grab another rope and tie her to. It took us a while and certainly wasn't very "yachty," but we more or less ended up where we wanted to. God only knows what the yachtsmen-observers thought.

Back to Tommy for a minute. A tall, slim, clean-shaven but scruffy-looking veteran, he was quite a character. We knew that he served in the Navy in the Pacific Theater in World War II, but we were never quite sure what he did—he would only say he was a cook, but we suspected more. Fritz owned a surplus PT Boat that he sometimes ran, and Tommy was always there to help him operate it. He was a first-rate guitar player and a very adept golf hustler, sometimes appearing like a bumpkin wearing no shoes and only three clubs—who would eventually clean out someone's wallet with side bets—an act repeated on the many Florida courses.

Anyway, back to the story of that first trip, when Tommy and I were the only two on board. Having cast off and under way, we were about to go under one of the Florida inland waterway bridges when I looked up and saw Fritz. He had come to see us off and to wave good-bye, and he was with the girl who had come to Florida with me! We looked up and waved, Fritz waved and the girl waved. All of a sudden, Fritz looked down at me, put his arm around her, smiled and said, "Don't worry, I'll take good care of her." Tommy thought that was hilarious, and he just kept laughing. I just stood there and thought, "Well, that's the last I'll see of her." And it was.

Off we sailed, out to sea, across the Gulf Stream, the intense, very strong, warm ocean current that moves north along the coast of Florida and then eventually across the Atlantic. We were so loaded up with freight—piles of split cedar shingles and other building supplies—that we didn't have any deck to walk on and had to walk on top of the cargo.

When we were in the Gulf Stream, Tommy was below in the engine room, and I was on top walking to the stern for something when the boat suddenly rolled a little bit one way, and I rolled the other way and then I was overboard. Luckily, I came up to the surface just in time to see in the corner of my eye some object going by, so I grabbed it—it was the dinghy we were towing. Pulling myself up into the small boat, I sat there and waited for about ten minutes for Tommy to emerge from the engine room. Needless to say, if I hadn't fortunately grabbed that dinghy, I would have been floating in the Gulf Stream for a long time. A really long time.

Eventually I watched as Tommy came up on deck, went into the wheelhouse, then walked around the boat looking for me, ending at the stern. When he finally spied me, he yelled, "Hey, Em, what are you doing back there?" I replied, "Don't worry about it—you drive your boat, and I'll drive mine!" Tommy got another big laugh out of that, and then he slowed down enough so that we could take up the slack between the two boats to allow me to re-board the *Seven Dwarfs*, without further incident.

Over time, Tommy, Bengt and I had many adventures involving that cargo ship. From the beginning, the routine was for us to transport a load of building materials to Providenciales, stay there while we all worked on building the Third Turtle Inn until we ran out of building supplies, then take the boat back and repeat the process. Needless to say, we made numerous trips, and I soon became the semi-permanent crew on the *Seven Dwarfs*. Quite a job responsibility for a bookkeeper.

As my local friend Sherlock Walkin from Blue Hills recalled years later, "When Provo first started off, there was nothing. I remember the *Seven Dwarfs*—when my granddaddy went up, he had a small boat with a horse power on it, and he went down to see Tommy Coleman." When

I arrived in the Islands, there were maybe 400 people on Provo; now, there are about 30,000.

Occasionally, Ray Ward would come along on one of these trips. Ray was the builder in charge—a contractor from Delray Beach. He was acquainted with all the local building problems in the islands and was experienced at "making do" with whatever you had. "When we started here…there were no skilled people on the Island," Tommy Coleman recalled, "Ray Ward was the man who trained all these people." Ray's son still works in the Islands as a contractor.

Billy Dodson, our heavy equipment operator, came along on one trip. Hailing from Texas, Billy was the "cat skinner" premier—he was proficient at handling bulldozers, graders and anything with Caterpillar treads.

On one occasion, Fritz Ludington wanted to build a road and an airport in Providenciales, so he just jumped on top of this D8 cat, a large track-type tractor-bulldozer, and gave directions to Billy, the operator. "Okay, Billy, go this way, go that way," he would yell at the top of his voice while hanging on, holding his arm out like you do when directing the navigator of a boat through rocky water. "This way, that way, right, left." Billy just put the ripper teeth down, went right through the bush and that was the first road. Although it's since been paved, that road is still in existence, still in the same place. So much for surveyors, engineers and laying designs out scientifically.

There was another incident involving me falling overboard on our travels—this one in The Cut—that is, the main cut—up in the Exumas. Regular sailors in the Exumas chain in the Bahamas know about the cuts. This chain of islands roughly runs northwest to southeast for just under 100 miles and is broken up by a series of cuts, or passes. In the Exumas, the cuts tend to be rather narrow, so the amount of water flowing through a cut can be quite impressive. Add a little wind opposing the current flow and you can very quickly develop dangerous seas with a vicious current, making for a dicey situation considering there is land on both sides of you.

Usually when leaving Nassau, we would sail down the inside of the bank for a while, then cut through and tie up in Georgetown to spend a few days there. This time it was pretty rough in the Cut, and the cargo was being tossed all over the deck. As usual, we were sinking—or seriously leaking. One of our main pumps wasn't working, so I fastened a gasoline-engine pump to the rail. While I was pulling and pulling, trying to start the damn thing, the rope broke and I went over backwards. Tommy thought that was hilarious, and he turned the *Dwarfs* around, threw me a rope and picked me up. Then we proceeded into Georgetown without further incident or dunking.

Generally, on these trips, we would leave Delray Beach, travel to Nassau, then stay there two or three days, celebrating our successful crossing of the Gulf Stream. Sometimes Fritz, Ray Ward or Bengt Söderqvist, the original surveyor of Turks and Caicos, would meet us in Nassau. Bengt's later job was to lay out and plan all the lots and roads on Provo.

We would just have one hell of a good time in Nassau, running around, drinking too much, dancing all night, chasing women and generally having one continual party. It was just the ideal life for a young, single guy like me. We'd go to bars such as Charlie's and Over the Hill and similar watering holes and night spots. Sometimes we would go down to the Exumas, stop in Georgetown and stay there a few days just to celebrate having gotten that far! At the time, that was Fritz's home, so that became our headquarters, and we'd end up staying there four or five days. After a few days of partying and carrying on, we would move on past Long Island, Aklins, Crooked, Mayaguana and finally into Providenciales, or "Blue Hills."

On one occasion, we arrived in Georgetown just in time for the Out Island Regatta, which was great timing on our part—it was quite a giant party, featuring sailboats from all over the Bahamas with visitors and tourists, everyone with wild partying on their minds. The Out Islands refer to all the islands in the Bahamas that are not Nassau.

Tommy always carried conch pearls which he had bought or traded from the local people in Providenciales. These are pearls that are found in conchs and are very pretty with a beautiful pink color—like the shade of a pink dogwood blossom—although they have an irregular shape.

Now, Tommy was always trying to barter these items to tourist women in exchange for spending the night with him. For the benefit of the woman he had his eye on, Tommy would play the role of the grizzled old salt, the veteran of the sea, saying, "Here, here, I got something I want to show you, got something I want to show you." He always kind of half-stuttered when he was coming on like this, then he'd pull out this old red rag, unwrap it in this dingy joint of Fritz's—the Two Turtles bar—and lay out these absolutely beautiful conch pearls. The women would gasp and respond, "Oh, aren't they beautiful, aren't they so beautiful? How can I get one of those?" Tommy would just smile, and reply, "Well you can have one of these." They'd ask, "Oh, yeah, how much is it?" Tommy would say, "Well, I won't sell it, but I might trade you something for it—whatcha got to trade?" with a big grin on his face. It always seemed like Tommy's approach was more successful than not because he almost always needed more conch pearls when we returned to Provo.

In recent years, conchs have become a very big deal in the Islands. Since 2004, Providenciales has hosted the Turks and Caicos Conch Festival—a celebration of the Islands' national symbol and top export—the marine snail that for years has played an integral role in local cuisine.

On another *Seven Dwarfs* trip, we were sailing between Crooked and Long Island when we started leaking—again. Evidently, there was a loose seal at the site where the engine shaft went through the hull of the boat. However, this time the main engine pump had quit, and we couldn't get our small pump to bail out the water to keep us afloat. Down in the engine room, I was working frantically, trying to figure out something to keep us afloat, but the sea water was already half way up the main engine, and we finally decided it was hopeless—we were going to sink.

So, we prepared our little dinghy by putting an outboard motor on it, along with food, water and all the other supplies that we might need for drifting around for a few days. We were not particularly worried about it at the time, as I recall; there was nothing to prevent abandoning the ship, so that's what we got ready to do—no big deal.

Well, we got the dinghy ready, but we decided that we'd just keep steaming towards Crooked Island for as long as we could in order to get closer to land. As we steamed straight for Bird Rock on Crooked Island, the northwest end, I believe, we were gradually sinking lower and lower, taking in more water. Finally, we sailed around the tip of Bird Rock, where a lighthouse was located on the little island—a rock, literally. And lo and behold, there was a freighter sitting there. Thinking, "Geez, thank God," we managed to close the distance to the freighter, and Tommy recognized the boat and its captain.

The captain of the Bahamian cargo boat was a Nassau fellow. His crew threw down some big hawsers to us, and we tied off the *Seven Dwarfs* to the side of the freighter to prevent us from sinking. Then they dropped down a big pump, and pumped us out. Making some additional repairs, we then went ashore on Crooked Island.

Upon landing, we discovered that there was some type of big political campaign taking place there in which we somehow got involved, but the details are murky. People were constantly asking us what party we were in and what we were going to do, and we would answer that "We were just passing through, man, just passing through."

Eventually we called Fritz on a radio telephone to report what happened, and his only comment was, "Well, you got it fixed?" When we answered "Yes," he replied,

"Well, come on, what are you waiting for?" Realizing that he was probably right, we set off again in the *Seven Dwarfs*, having gotten the packing around the shaft redone—the shaft that went from the engine through the hull of the boat. The vessel was in fair shape, so we sailed on. Completing the rest of the trip, we passed by Mayaguana and Provo, tying up at our official address: Heaving Down Rock, Providenciales, Turks and Caicos Islands.

Mayaguana is the most easterly island of the Bahamas, and was the starting point for still another high-seas adventure on the *Seven Dwarfs*. That was the time when Tommy and I left there for Provo carrying an automobile that was secured over the front hatch. We did not realize that the metal in the car was disrupting our compass. Going from island to island, we eventually ran out of islands and saw no more land.

At some point, we were sighted by Fritz in his plane, flying low to point us in the right direction to Provo. He later told us that we were on course to sail to Africa. We were certainly navigationally-challenged, in today's parlance.

Another time, we had a very enjoyable trip down to the Islands with our usual stops: Nassau, Georgetown, and so on. Up to a point. As it was getting dark, we sailed into Abrahams Bay—we never travelled at night because we never knew where we were in the dark. In the darkness, we couldn't see the next island and we didn't want to chance running into any reefs that weren't visible.

Well, we spent a quiet night after tying up in Abrahams Bay and didn't see anyone after we arrived. There was plenty to eat because we always carried canned foods. Fritz had torn out the old galley of the boat so there would be more room for cargo, so we would take a can of deboned chicken or beans or whatever and hold it next to the engine stack so it would warm up. Sometimes we would stop on an uninhabited island, such as Samana Cay, use driftwood to build a fire and then make supper. This was how we ate when we were at sea.

The following day, we left Abrahams Bay and got about ten miles out when the storm blew up. A big one. It was just terrible—we had green water coming right over the bow and smashing into the wheelhouse. Up in the pointy end of the boat, as Tommy called it, there was a small forward hatch that led to the old galley space, and the cover for that hatch suddenly just washed away and disappeared as a wave crashed over the bow.

Tommy looked at me, and I looked at him and we decided that we better fix the thing before it flooded us. Tommy said, "You better fix it, Em!" I replied, "What do you mean, ME?" His response was, "I'm the captain!" So I went to work. Somehow, I got a piece of plywood from somewhere, maybe a cabinet door, along with a hammer and some nails. There I was, crawling up the deck, holding on to this piece of plywood, with the hammer literally in my teeth.

When I finally reached the blown hatch, I wrapped myself around the Samson post, a strong 10x10 pillar fixed to the deck, and used as a support for the ropes, tackle or other equipment, with my legs and started trying to nail down this sheet of plywood. The boat was pitching horribly from side to side, and I could only get one nail hammered in by the time another big wave hit us. We must have been in 12- or 15-foot seas. So then I'd get another couple of nails in and wham! An even larger wave would strike us. Holding my breath, wrapping my legs tighter around that post, gripping the hammer and nails, waiting till we came up again, I managed to hammer in a few more nails.

Occasionally I'd look up and see Tommy laughing away—he thought this was just great fun! At last I succeeded in getting the plywood cover nailed on, and, wet to the bone, I managed to safely crawl back into the wheelhouse.

At that point, we thought we had better call Fritz to see if he was in a big hurry, or if it was OK for us to return to Abrahams Bay. Fritz was in South Caicos when we reached him on the radio, and we advised him that we were in the middle of a big storm, it was chaotic and we weren't sure what direction we were headed anyway since he automatic pilot wasn't working. Fritz, his usual self, said, "Oh, don't worry about it, it's just a little squall line, come on through, you'll clear it in another five or ten miles."

It was more like another five hours or so when we finally cleared that storm! I suppose our navigation skills weren't that bad because we could see Blue Mountain on Providenciales when we broke through. Blue Mountain, I was told, is the highest point between Haiti and Florida, with an elevation of 156 feet. So, we sailed on, coming through the cut in the North Reef and tying up at our dock at Leeward Beach. Safe to sail another day.

Chapter 4: Building the Third Turtle

Geographically, the Turks and Caicos Islands are situated on the southern end of the Bahamas archipelago. Having a multitude of beautiful, white-sand beaches, the Islands looked to me just like part of the Bahamas, which lie just about 60 miles to the northwest. Situated some 100 miles to the north of Haiti and the Dominican Republic—and about 575 miles southeast of Miami—Turks and Caicos were low and dry with not much soil. The fishing was not very good, although the snorkeling and diving was tremendous. The color of the coastal water and the offshore coral reefs was simply stunning.

The country was divided into two main island groups, totaling only about 166 square miles of land: To the west were the Caicos Islands—West Caicos, Providenciales, North Caicos, Middle Caicos, East Caicos, South Caicos and over 30 cays. A cay (pronounced "key") is a small, low-elevation, sandy island. South Caicos was the commercial center of the Islands when I arrived on the scene in 1966. Tina Fulford Barron, from an old South Caicos family, commented, "South Caicos was like a standard—we had the upper class, the middle class, the in-between class and the lower class."

To the east were the Turks Islands—Grand Turk, Salt Cay and nine uninhabited cays. These two groups of islands were separated by a 22-mile wide—and 7,000 feet deep—channel of water called the Columbus Passage; it was better known by the locals as Turks Islands Passage.

Nowadays, many tourists visit the Passage every January through March to watch thousands of humpback whales migrate to their mating grounds. When I first lived there in the '60s and '70s, I was aware of this migration and sometimes saw whales while I was flying for Caicos Airways. In the last 15 years or so, the number of tourists has greatly increased; some come on ships to view them, and some people travel to Grand Turk to go out on local boats. It's really amazing. Once, maybe in 2007, with only a mask, snorkel and flippers, I went out swimming with the whales. Looking directly into one's eye, I realized that it was strange to be so close to something so huge. They were very peaceful animals.

The Bermudians originally settled the Turks and Caicos in the 1600s in order to produce salt. They imported slaves from Africa and originated the salt industry, which functioned through manual labor for 300 years. The workers employed windmill—with wooden gears so as not to rust—gravity and tides to do their work. It was impossible at that time to import steel or iron. My friend Oswald "King Oz" Francis, a well-known resident—and former lighthouse keeper—from Grand Turk explained, "The main industry was salt…we had hundreds of mules doing the salt because the horses couldn't do it—they would get ground itch. We shipped salt the entire year."

Francis went on to explain that locals received more pay working at the U.S. Navy's so-called North Base after its arrival in 1954, and they didn't want to think about working salt for the Turks Island Salt Company (TISCO). "We had the fishing salt and the table salt," he explained, "In the ponds, the pay wasn't much—the men in the ponds would go there early in the morning and rake salt."

When I arrived in 1966, the salt industry in the Islands was staggering. It completely collapsed shortly thereafter due to a lack of mechanization and manpower. Sea captain Percy Talbott, a friend of mine from Salt Cay, confirmed that during my interview with him many years later: "When

Embry arrived...there wasn't much salt being shipped from the Islands. There was little salt being shipped to Jamaica; the salt business failed in Grand Turk and South Caicos; and, it couldn't keep the three Islands going. TISCO couldn't continue like that. So, the salt business was left only in Salt Cay, and eventually that ended altogether." My friend Norman Saunders from South Caicos, a long-time politician who would later become Chief Minister of the Turks and Caicos, added, "(the salt industry) was officially replaced with the lobster industry."

However, it appears that there may be a renewed interest in the commercial salt industry due to the current popularity of sea salt in the United States.

For years, Turks and Caicos was classified as a British Crown colony, in the same governance group as Bermuda, the Bahamas and Jamaica. After the Bahamas were granted independence in 1973, the Islands became a British Overseas Territory. About 32,000 people populate the Turks and Caicos now, as compared to the 5,000 or so locals during my ten years of activity there.

When I first arrived, there were zero tourists from stateside and no cruise lines operating nearby; however, Providenciales is now a major tourist destination, and Carnival and other cruise lines have made Grand Turk a port of choice. In my early days in the Islands, there were few attractions that would interest someone from outside the islands.

One of the recognizable exceptions was Fritz Ludington's Third Turtle Inn. Fritz's original Two Turtles Inn—located on Exuma in the Bahamas—had become quite successful. Since that watering hole had a lot of name recognition, he decided to stick with a similar brand and concept for constructing his newest venture in the Turks and Caicos, situated in the middle of the north coast of Provo.

Although I didn't know beans about construction, building the Third Turtle was quite a lot of fun. Upon my arrival, Ray Ward the contractor had a conversation with me that went like this:

Ray: "You're now a foreman on the building crew."

Me (truthfully): "But I don't know anything about building."

Ray (quickly): "You don't have to know anything about building. These guys, local fellows, know how to pour concrete and set forms and all that kind of stuff."

Me (sincerely): "Well, what am I supposed to do?"

Ray: "You're just supposed to stand around and be white and try not to show that you don't know anything. They'll figure that since you're white, you'll know what you're doing."

So, I just stood around being white most of the time, made myself somewhat useful and, as it turned out, I learned a lot about construction. Ray's insightful remarks truly reflected the attitude of the Islands at that time.

Fritz had decided that we needed modern, reliable transportation on Provo, so on one of the *Dwarfs* trips, we brought along an old made-in-the USA, World War II, Army-surplus Jeep. Up to that time, there were no roads on the Island and no vehicles. People travelled to their destination by either foot, sailboat or one of the only two boats on the Island powered by outboard motor. As we unloaded the Jeep, we thought it would be a great help because we'd be able to haul materials from Leeward Beach, which was several long miles from where we were constructing the Third Turtle. Leeward Beach is one of the best beaches on Providenciales, and it can be accessed at the Leeward Going Through point, a place where the currents can become a little tricky.

Shortly after that, I drove our trusty, dependable Jeep over what appeared to be some brush, but an old rock was buried in those bushes—I tore up the transmission pretty badly. Luckily, Bill Dodson managed to fix it. Hailing from Texas, Billy was a tall (6'0"), slim (120 pounds) heavy equipment operator who worked for Provident, Ltd. Billy was involved in his own flight misadventure once when the handles broke off the control wheel when he was landing his Cessna 182. He had to totally use his manual dexterity to grab the hub of the control wheel and manipulate it in order to land safely.

There was another amusing incident involving the Jeep and me, but it will take a while for me to get to the punchline. Officially, I was still the bookkeeper for Provident, Ltd. My duties and directions mainly consisted of Fritz giving me the checkbook, saying, "Now you keep track of what's going on, and write checks when you need to, and mark down in columns whether the expense is for building materials, transport, airplanes, living expenses or whatever." So that's what I would do.

On one occasion, Fritz and I went to Nassau to buy some heavy equipment for the construction project. Now, my check-writing days in college and in the Army had been limited to $5.00 or so, maybe $15.00 at the most on a big weekend. So when Fritz, who was doing all the negotiating to buy this equipment, turned to me and said "Alright, Em, write them a check for $80,000.00," I just about dropped my pants! I didn't know that we had that much in the account, and of course we didn't. However, Fritz planned to make a large deposit before the check cleared.

Anyway, we closed the deal and arranged for an LCT-type landing craft to travel from Nassau to Provo transporting all that heavy equipment. Among the purchases were a D8 cat—the large track-type tractor-bulldozer that I mentioned earlier—a dragline crane, a road grader, a pickup truck and a front-end loader.

Well, the locals in Provo had never seen anything like this. In fact, the entire Island was at the beach to meet and greet us—even all the teachers and children were out of school to view this "historic event!" The young ones only related to boats and sailing as a form of transportation. When their teachers assigned them the task of writing stories and drawing pictures of their impressions of the D8 cat bulldozer being offloaded, all the drawings they made were fascinating due to their marine orientation. For example, one young boy drew a picture of a bulldozer with a sail on it; another picture showed a flag from the "stern" of the bulldozer. In short, it was a big deal, a very big deal, and it represented a rapid and significant change in the lives of those native Islanders. It's not for me to say whether it was a good change or not—I don't know that answer—only to accurately relate what happened.

My friend Sherlock Walkin from Blue Hills was just a little kid then, but he recalled that scene well: "I remember running around, looking and peeping. The old people used to call the bulldozer 'wild hogs.'" Sherlock became a successful entrepreneur and was the most prominent boat dealer in the Islands. In fact, I bought one from him.

To return to the story that I promised a few paragraphs earlier: The offloading of the pickup truck meant that there was another passenger vehicle on the Island in addition to the Jeep. Sure enough, with two vehicles and one road— actually a 6-8-foot pathway used as a road—it didn't take long for there to be a head-on collision—Fritz in the truck and me in the Jeep! Of course, Fritz loved to repeat that story to everyone he met: "Here's Embry and me, you know, the only two vehicles on the entire Island..."

For the next few months, things were really busy. I was doing a little bookkeeping, which was fairly rudimentary, as you may have guessed, and a lot of construction, which involved much travelling back and forth over the Island. Of course, we'd occasionally whoop it up and celebrate our hard labor over at South Caicos. Maybe once a month, Fritz would come in and announce, "Okay, boys, we're gonna go party!" And he'd get all of us into his Beechcraft Baron and ask, "Okay, where do you want to go? Nassau, Kingston, San Juan, Port-au-Prince, Santo Domingo? We'll whoop it up for the weekend." Fritz's Baron was a twin-engine, 6-seat aircraft that he used to fly between Florida, where he had moved, and various island destinations. It was no stranger to Georgetown, Great Exuma; Turks and Caicos; Port-au-Prince, Haiti; Santo Domingo, Dominican Republic; San Juan, Puerto Rico; and other Caribbean destinations.

Anyway, we'd pick someplace to party for the weekend, travel there, settle in and start having fun. For example, one time when we arrived in Santo Domingo, we hailed a taxi outside the airport and said, "Driver, take us to the finest hotel in town." So he took us to the Embajador—now known as the Occidental Hotel El Embajador—a 5-star hotel which was really nice. Fritz checked everybody in—two in a room—then we ate dinner. After that, we would typically hail another taxi and say, "Okay, driver, take us to the nightclubs." And Tommy Coleman would typically chime in and say, "Nightclubs, hell, take us to the 'ho-house.'" Anyway, we'd party, whoop it up and have a great time for a few days, then return to Provo for work, all hung over and feeling miserable.

In June of 1967, a major family event took place in Geneva, Switzerland when my brother Rudy, 21, married Sylvia Bogsch—their paths crossed when they were both attending Swarthmore College. Taking time off from my duties in the Islands, I flew TWA to Europe and had a great time.

An amusing incident occurred when I laid over in London on my way to that wedding. Just on a lark, I dropped into the Colonial Office, which was responsible for the administration of all British territories outside the British Isles. Politely, I asked the clerk who waited on me if he had any information about the Turks and Caicos. He looked at me in a very quizzical manner, whereupon I stated, "It's one of your colonies." Quickly he shot back, "Atlantic or Pacific?" So much for the stature and renown of the Islands.

Fritz and I managed to log a lot of flying time together. In 1967, he purchased a North American AT-6, better known as the T-6 Texan, a single-engine advanced trainer aircraft used to train pilots of many armed services from World War II into the 1970s. We picked it up at Kip Dupont's Summit Aviation in Delaware, and our destination was the Palm Beach County Airpark in Delray Beach, Florida. No sooner were we on our way when we both discovered that our usually faithful compasses were no longer working. What to do? Fritz said, "Keep flying, just keep the (Atlantic) Ocean on the left, and we'll eventually hit Florida." We would stop at various airports along the way, and Fritz would direct me, "Em, go out to the parking lot and check the license plates on the cars, because I don't want to have to ask what state we are in."

On another occasion around the same year, in a bar in Ft. Lauderdale, Florida, Fritz introduced me to a guy he said was Johnny Weissmüller, the famous Olympic swimmer and actor who played Tarzan in the 1930s and '40s. That story may have been true—Fritz said that Weissmüller was always hanging around there. In fact, I learned that the actor retired in 1965 and moved to Fort Lauderdale where he was Founding Chairman of the International Swimming Hall of Fame, and that he lived there until 1973. So, it may well have been him.

The best part was—I was getting paid for all this fun! My salary was $300 a month plus my living expenses; since I was single and had no dependents to worry about, that was all the money I needed. At that point in my life, I really had no major goal—I was just enjoying an interesting lifestyle; plus, my parents were never negative about me being there.

Tommy Coleman later summarized the results of our work: "The Third Turtle was built and opened in 1967, and the tourists started to come…People had never heard of the Turks and Caicos until we started this tourism industry here. We were island social climbers."

During the months that I was supervising, building and working on the construction of the Third Turtle, I wasn't doing any flying, and I was beginning to wonder when I'd get the opportunity to do so again. Then one day, a seaplane—a little single-engine Aeronca that had been converted to a float-plane by adding floats instead of wheels—came whizzing over the Island, circling it a few times. That was an unusual enough occurrence for everyone to stop working and take a good, long look up in the air. The seaplane eventually landed in the water right in front of where we were working, then it taxied slowly up to the beach as we all walked down to greet it. The cockpit door flew open, and out jumped a guy named Lew Whinnery.

That event was the beginning of our airline service and how I became involved in full-time flying.

Chapter 5: Jumping the Donkey

> *"The best pilots fly more than the others;*
> *that's why they're the best."*
> —*Chuck Yeager*

Lewis A. "Lew" Whinnery was a pleasant, charming guy and quite a character. When I asked him where he was from, he answered "Up north." When I asked him where he had just flown from, he replied casually, "Oh, I been down in Guyana." He went on to explain that he had been mining in the rivers down there and was returning with his bag of diamonds. I excitedly inquired, "How many diamonds do you have?" Answering that question, he pulled out a large bag which he said was filled with diamonds—pounds and pounds of them. In fact, I never knew whether they were worth a hundred dollars or a million dollars, because they stayed in that sack and I never saw them—and I'm fairly certain that Lew never did either. From experience, I knew that the Islands at that time attracted a variety of dreamers, con-artists and bull-shitters.

Naturally, one thing led to another—Fritz being interested in all types of aircraft but specially fascinated with the seaplane, and Lew being a self-described adventurer—and pretty soon Lew decided to base his operations in South Caicos to make a living, just like us. His plan was to begin an air taxi service with his seaplane and carry people back and forth to Grand Turk and other nearby islands. Somewhere along the line either Lew sold his valuable diamonds or something else mysterious occurred, because they disappeared—if they ever existed.

As it turned out, Lew was broke. That's how Fritz wound up financing the next stage of this air taxi endeavor. His wife Chris flew a Cessna 180 tail dragger that carried a pilot and three passengers, so Fritz brought that plane down to the islands for the air taxi business since the seaplane was not dependable in rough weather and choppy water. The Cessna 180 was a fixed conventional gear, general aviation plane which was produced between 1953 and 1981.

Planes were called tail-draggers when they had a small wheel under the tail of the plane rather than a larger one under the nose. Since I had never flown a tail-wheel plane before then, Fritz checked me out in it to make sure I could handle it. Such aircraft are quite different from other planes because they are more difficult to land and in the way they handle on the ground. Today, most pilots never fly one because they've basically disappeared from general use; they're mostly used as bush planes for landing on sandbars or in the rough fields of Alaska or Canada. They can handle rougher surfaces without fear of the nose-wheel breaking and the engine then plowing into the ground.

Anyway, in a short while, we also acquired an Aztec; by that time, I was just itching to fly one of these airplanes, which I thought would be great. The Piper PA-23, first named Apache and later Aztec, was a six-seat, twin-engine light aircraft, manufactured from 1952 to 1981.

As I said, that's how I ended up going over to South Caicos to work with Lew on the air service. Lew had checked me out in the Cessna 180, so I ferried people around in that. Make no mistake: With only perhaps 300 flying hours at the time, I still wasn't any big-time hotshot pilot. However, I truly enjoyed flying. And, although I never flew Lew's Aeronca, I did eventually obtain a seaplane rating from an instructor in Miami Beach.

With consistent easterly trade winds, the Turks and Caicos Islands in general had a very pleasant climate and weather, other than the occasional passing hurricane or tropical storm. For most of the year, there was a constant 8 to 10 to 15 mph cooling breeze from the east. When that breeze died down in October, the temperature was in the 90s, but humidity was never a big factor. After a while, you just got used to the heat. It only rained an average of 13 inches per year.

Visitors thought the temperature and cooling winds were great—but then discovered they were sunburned red after an hour! A really cool day in wintertime meant that the temperature went down to 69 degrees—and all the locals wore coats and hats due to the cold weather.

Anyway, one of my first taxi-trips was for Robin Wainwright, the Administrator of the Islands, and for the local Legislative Council. My assignment involved ferrying them in the Cessna, one load at a time, from Grand Turk to Providenciales so they could see the progress of the construction development.

Robin was an acquaintance of mine who was a British Army veteran of World War II. I first met him in England in 1967. After the war, he moved to British Kenya and operated a farm there with his brother, only to lose everything during the Mau Mau uprising in the 1950s that left many people dead, much property destroyed and the country devastated. At that point, he joined the British Colonial Service and was ultimately assigned to Turks and Caicos.

The local Council was comprised of nine or ten locals, some appointed and some elected from each Island; most were very unsophisticated. Sometimes we disagreed over what I thought were simple issues—such as the time I found it necessary to raise their airfares due to an increase in fuel costs, and they just didn't want to pay more.

Now, this was before we had the permanent airstrip built; at the time, we only had a little 800-foot landing strip where the locals had cut all the brush down and removed the big rocks. Gustavus "Gustav" Lightbourne recalled, "The first airstrip was built around '66 or '67—this was called the 'Machete Airport.'" That's what the locals used to clear the field.

On my first landing approach with the officials on board, I had everything lined up perfectly, when all of a sudden, I let my air speed get too slow and—WHAM! The plane just slammed into the ground. Calming my passengers down, I nonchalantly explained to them that that was the way we landed there because we had to stop in a hurry since the landing strip was so short. My explanation seemed to float right by them without controversy.

The only real work I faced from that booming landing was repairing one wheel that had a couple of cracks in it; eventually, I just replaced it. The other minor issue was a hole in the horizontal stabilizer, no doubt caused by a rock that flew up during the landing. That was a simple fix. Taking an old metal oil can, I patched it onto the hole with pop rivets. It was good as new.

George Ewing from South Caicos, a descendant of early salt proprietors, and Evan Wood from Grand Turk were two important members of the Legislative Council at that time; and, when I flew them to Provo, it was the first time they had ever visited there. That showed me how out-of-touch most lawmakers and politicians were with other regions in the Islands.

Good news: In practically no time, our air taxi service became very popular. We ran daily scheduled flights from South Caicos to Grand Turk and occasionally to Providenciales. Not surprisingly, I was beginning to connect with the locals. It helped that I could identify locals from different villages based on their physical and facial appearance alone. Another interesting marvel: The locals absolutely never became airsick during a flight; I believe that this held true because they never heard of anyone else ever getting sick and didn't know that sometimes airsickness happened. Occasionally, after a longer flight, my passengers would cheer and clap loudly when we successfully landed.

Meanwhile, I had moved to South Caicos. I rented a room from Captain and Mrs. Stanley Malcolm who lived right across from the Anglican Church, a location I was acutely aware of every Sunday morning as the large church bell clanged away a mere 20 feet from my bed. He was the Captain of the *Sea Horse*, the old government launch that made a daily journey to Grand Turk in the morning and returned to South Caicos at night. The Sea Horse was popularly known as the Vomit Comet.

It was really sort of a bizarre housing arrangement. My living space was this tiny room which hung out over the street about three feet; in some places, the rafters were only six feet high, in others they were 8 to 10 feet high. Of course, there was no electricity or running water—all I had was a kerosene lamp, a chamber pot under the bed and a basin of water and a towel for washing up. After an evening at the Admiral's Arms bar, one of my favorite night spots, I would return to my room to undress before going to bed and light the lamp. Inevitably, I would later forget that the lamp was hot, pick up the globe to blow it out and burn my fingers. Believe me, I lived with burned fingers quite a bit.

Each morning, Mrs. Malcolm always made me breakfast—a thermos of hot water and some instant coffee, usually a boiled egg and some toast with her delicious homemade bread. Then, Captain Malcolm and I would walk down to the dock together each day, and he would board the *Sea Horse* and take it over to Grand Turk, a trip that took about four hours. Meanwhile, after parting ways with him, I would jump on my new 200cc Honda dirt bike which I bought on a trip to Florida, race out to the airport, take off in my plane and make my 14-minute flight to Grand Turk—flying there and back about 8 times each day.

At night, the two of us would both arrive home at about the same time and discuss our day's experience. It was really quite interesting—the complete opposite poles of travel, the old and the new. The Captain and I got along splendidly with each other.

A brief note about motorcycles: In high school, I often rode a 1948 74ci Indian Chief, which I borrowed from Harold "Hal" Taylor, Assistant Minister at St. Francis in the Fields. Go figure! Then, when I was a student at Kenyon College, I bought a Zündapp, a motorcycle from an old-line German manufacturer. Many years later, around 1979, I moved on to a couple of great big Harleys for a few years.

My Harley-riding occurred many years before the renewed popularity of that bike among baby boomers in the 1990s, and I was never involved in any bad crashes. A Kentuckty State Trooper did stop me once when I was riding my Harley on US 42 in Prospect—I was accelerating and it got a bit noisy. He commented, "Ain't you a little old for this sort of thing?"

Anyhow, that South Caicos Honda dirt bike was a favorite of mine for years; that and a Honda 500cc that I owned when we later lived in Haiti.

About this time, we were fortunate to receive the official contract to deliver mail in the Islands. However, since there was no way to land at the villages in North Caicos or Middle Caicos, we had a delivery problem. We solved it by just circling the post office in the village until we attracted someone's attention, then we'd open a window and throw out the bag of mail. Occasionally, we would also make similar food drops of unbreakable containers and items. This was great aerial service, but in one direction only, since we couldn't figure out any way to rig up a mail bag pickup with a hook so that we could snatch it up from the air. We decided that the answer was to build some more airstrips, and so we did.

"Speed" Gardiner from North Caicos recalled those days: "Embry used to drop the mail off by plane. The postman was Mr. Bob Williams. One time they couldn't locate the mail bag. So, they sent all the children from the school in search of the mail and offered a reward to whomever found it."

The incident he described may have been the one that generated an angry letter that postmaster Bob sent me. It went: "Dear Captain Embry, From now on, drop the mailbag at the base of the flagpole, not out in the rough" and so forth. With all due respect to Bob, he showed his lack of familiarity with my many tasks—I had to fly a plane going 80 mph, and maintain control while I pushed a mail bag out. Hitting his preferred target was not always my main concern.

During 1969-70, there was a lot of excitement surrounding the activity on South Caicos when the British Royal Engineers were assigned to make improvements to the runway there. This entire military operation became the source of great entertainment for the locals. Their version of the PX, or Post Exchange, offered duty-free alcohol, which caught the attention of everyone.

There was an amusing incident early on when the Engineers were arriving. A snobbish advance guy from the Royal Air Force (RAF) approached a local named Zaputa, whose job was to refuel the planes. "Yes, what you want?" asked Zaputa. The RAF guy said condescendingly, "Great silver bird come today." Zaputa, who had refilled countless airplanes of all types, sarcastically replied, "What you want me to do with great silver bird? Put in special fuel?"

A substantial number of remarkably strange things that later make great stories happened during my flying days in the Islands. Once, someone excitedly reported to me, "Plane coming in with no motor!" That was true—a glider was approaching. The glider landed, followed by the tow plane. They were part of a "riders in a glider" tour originating in the Virgin Islands. The couple was really funny—the man introduced his wife to me as Pussy Galore, after the James Bond character in *Goldfinger*. Later, I learned that she was actually a top acrobatic pilot.

One of the most frightening flying incidents happened in the early 1970s when I was chartered to fly a dead body from Grand Turk to Nassau, about 450 miles. The rather large body bag extended from the rear seat to the front, right next to me. After takeoff, I started climbing above the weather when I felt something in the bag nudging my elbow! It was so startling, right out of the blue. Immediately I yelled "WTF!" And then it happened again! Finally, after controlling my alarm and accompanying panic, I deduced that, as the airplane climbed from sea level, the altitude had caused the bag to expand in size, which in turn had caused the enclosed body parts to shift. What a flight that was.

On one occasion, Lew and I took a young fellow, Albert "Butch" Clare, from South Caicos on one of our mail runs to Middle Caicos, the largest of the islands in the Turks and Caicos. Butch's older brother was Bill Clare, a local customs agent, and they were part of a prominent family in South Caicos. Butch, about 16 years old then, used to help us out by doing odd jobs around the airstrip when planes arrived. We took him along because he enjoyed flying, and we thought that he could help us chop brush on the landing strip. Butch later became a photographer on a large cruise ship, and then studied hotel management; he is now the manager of one of the large hotels on the Islands. It was around 2010 that I last saw him there.

Well, we landed on the beach near the village of Conch Bar, the largest of the three towns in Middle Caicos, met with the villagers there and told them that we could start regular mail pick-up service if they would only clear out a little more brush and make the landing strip slightly longer. To accomplish this, we bought them some machetes, demonstrated what needed to be done and left. About three days later we returned and, sure enough, there was a usable airstrip, and we were able to start mail service to that location.

Now, for Lorimers, a town located in the northeast middle end of the Island—that lone airstrip wasn't effective for *their* delivery; because no road connected Conch Bar to Lorimers. In fact, there weren't roads connecting any of the villages on Middle Caicos. Fortunately for us, there was competition between the locals. In a short while, the Lorimers villagers agreed that a sand bar out in the middle of the bay would work, so they cleared the brush from it, and that was *their* airport. That was not an ideal solution for several practical reasons: First, the villagers had to walk about a half-mile from their town to the water and then pole their boats about another half-mile across the bay to reach the sand bar where we landed. However, *we* still enjoyed great traffic in and out of there, on two new airstrips.

The entire area was extremely primitive and undeveloped. "When I left Middle Caicos, there was no vehicle there, not even a bicycle," recalled Islander Cardinal Arthur, a cave guide from Middle Caicos. "Sometime in '69 vehicles arrived. Before that, all we had were donkeys, so we used to use that as transportation between Conch Bar, Lorimers and Bambara. When I came back in '75, there were vehicles."

The last village in Middle Caicos to clear out an airstrip for us was Bambara. Located east of Conch Bar about half a mile inland, this village is the second largest settlement on Middle Caicos. It is notable as the only town in the Turks and Caicos Archipelago that has a name of African derivation; the Bambara tribe is from the West African country of Mali. The village was probably first settled by survivors of the Spanish slave ship *Trouvadore* that sank off the coast in 1842.

Coincidentally, in about 2002, a group doing research on the *Trouvadore* came to the Islands. Needing a boat to pull a large magnetometer that they were using to look for its wreckage, they ended up borrowing my Boston Whaler.

The area around Conch Bar in Middle Caicos has long been noted for its cave system, which extends directly to the ocean. In those limestone caves in the 1880s, the

British used to mine guano, the waste droppings of birds and bats, used as a highly effective fertilizer. Today, Conch Bar Caves National Park is the site of the largest above-water cave system in the West Indies.

So, it turned out that there were three airstrips on the island within a space of about 10 miles, with no connecting road between the villages. Some days, we would have to deliver or pick up mail at all three locations—one after the other, up and down, up and down. It was just like driving a bouncing bus over one of their rough roads. My friend Sherlock Walkin recalled, "The first roads we had built, they used cracked rocks—then the ladies would bring the red mud and spread it over the road."

With the kind of mail and taxi service that we were operating, we had to be ready for the unexpected to happen; and, whatever snafus we encountered, we needed to be ready to solve them ourselves, because there was no one else around to do it for us. One of those unforeseen things happened to me at Lorimers.

Since I was supposed to pick up some passengers there, I was flying a Beechcraft Twin Bonanza, a pretty large airplane—I think it was a B50 model with two 275 HP engines. There were only 139 of these built. It would hold three in the front and three in the next seat, plus we had installed a seat from a wrecked Cessna 172 in the rear luggage compartment and that enabled us to hold two additional folks. Those passengers didn't have visibility to the side but could see forward over the other seats. Of course, that seat wasn't even fastened down to the floor—it was just shoved into that space. There just weren't any aviation laws or regulations that governed us at that time, and no inspections to concern us.

Remember that this was the little airstrip on the sandbar which was about 700 to 800 feet long. After setting down there, I left the plane and waited for the passengers to arrive from the nearby town. Because I was early and had some time on my hands, I stretched out in the shade of the wing of the plane, propped my head up and promptly fell asleep.

When I finally awoke a little later, there was all manner of jabbering and chattering from the crowd of people who had assembled. Unfortunately, I had landed close to high tide, the sea was coming in and the airplane was sinking into the soft sand at a quick rate—already maybe 10 to 12 inches. In fact, all three wheels were well into the sand, and the propellers were almost touching the ground!

The assembled local multitude was engaged in a great discussion about what I was going to do—pull it out, push it out, or just sit back and let the plane sink there and rot. Then an idea hit me, and I went into action, to save both my plane and my pride.

Persuading some bystanders to round up some shovels, we first dug three trenches, one in front of each wheel, each ditch going straight ahead and parallel to each other, for the wheels to roll in. Then we scraped out a small depression in front of each propeller, two more places going straight ahead and parallel to each other, where I figured the propellers were going to run. A few more onlookers were convinced to sit in the back of the plane to balance it and to hold the tail down. At that point, I started to pull the nose gear out by applying full power and hauling back on the plane's elevator; finally, that wheel came unglued and the back end went down. Once the nose wheel became freed, the main wheels ran through the ditches we had dug, up through the sand, and off we went!

After that unnerving occurrence, whenever I landed at Lorimers I quickly picked up my passengers and took off before that scene repeated itself. Once was enough.

Another one of those unpredicted events happened when I flew into Grand Turk and picked up a male passenger who was around 85 years old. Originally from Bambara, he had come to Grand Turk by sailboat and had been hospitalized for a while. When he entered the airplane, which was on the airstrip in the middle of Grand

Turk, I immediately noticed something unusual about his appearance. With his oilskin coat packed, his sweater on and carrying food and water, he was ready for a *sailboat* trip.

From experience, my passenger knew how long it took to reach Middle Caicos—just 30 miles away—and he was ready to hunker down. Not bothering to dissuade him of his misconception, I just told him that this trip wouldn't take long. In response, he just rested in the rear passenger seat and smiled back at me—he knew damn well how long the journey was, he'd been making it by sail for 85 years. He knew that the sea dropped off to 7,000 feet deep not long after leaving Grand Turk, making the currents very rough for some sailing vessels.

Well, about 15 minutes after departure, we landed in Bambara on a little airstrip that we had built on his land while he was in the hospital. He grabbed his belongings, left the plane, looked around and said, "This is land I farm on. How'd we get here?" Honest to God, he really did not know what had happened—he may have thought it was magic of some type!

The rest of the story is pretty neat too: He sincerely enjoyed the trip so much that every time he collected a few bucks—or five pounds Jamaican—he would come down and see me to take another flight!

When I interviewed Elizabeth "Titta" Forbes in 2005, she listened to that story and commented, "That was my uncle, John Saunders!"

The experience of her Uncle John showed the lack of familiarity of the locals with travel other than by boat. Norman Saunders, my friend from South Caicos who was born in 1943, said, "For moving about, we used the boat until Embry came along. All travel was by boat. I hated those January trips traveling back to school, as the seas were very rough during that time."

Speaking of dollars, the money situation in the Islands was somewhat unusual in that a mixture of many currencies was used. When I first arrived, it was not unusual to deal in Jamaican dollars, Jamaican pounds, Bahamian dollars—every tourist must have departed taking the unusual $3 Bahamian bill home—and U.S. dollars. Over time, the U.S. dollar became preferred and dominates the money scene today. Charles Misick, a friend from Bottle Creek in North Caicos recalled, "When we changed the money from Jamaican—(Liam) Maguire was here then. He was the one who push for the change from Jamaica currency to U.S. dollars. That was one of the best things to happen." Charles also worked as the North Caicos ticket agent for us. More about Liam in a later chapter.

In reality, the Grand Turk airstrip from which we took off was not what most people would call an airstrip—it was a local road, still in use. Church Folly Street ran approximately 1500 feet from the power lines to the cemetery. There was a prison located between Front Street and Pond Street, the latter named after all the salt ponds in the area. Right next to this lockup, at the front edge of the landing field, were power lines that ran about 20 feet high. Once I passed over the jail and the wires, I would have to drop and land very quickly because at the other end, only 1500 feet away, was the solid wall of the cemetery. We always thought it was very appropriate—if a pilot didn't successfully make the takeoff or landing, he'd end up in the right place.

Regarding that prison, my friend Oswald Francis from Grand Turk observed, "When you were put into prison, it was hard labor—you had to crack stones all day. They also used the cat-o-nine-tails...The meals were nothing compared to what they get today."

On our fairly small island—Grand Turk is seven miles long and one mile wide—we would also have to share that runway with cars, trucks and the occasional donkey or cow. Which brings me to the tale of Mr. Max Karant, Vice-President of the Aircraft Owner and Pilots Association (AOPA) and founder of the *AOPA Pilot* magazine, of which he was the editor for 18 years.

Max came through the Turks and Caicos several times, always flying his faithful Piper Pa-30 Twin Comanche, a four-seater with two small but reliable engines. Many pilots now only fly single engine aircraft because the turbine engines are so reliable, but that wasn't the case when Max flew.

Max was passing through the Islands as part of his research for a story in the magazine about flying in the West Indies. Seeking me out, we met in the Admiral's Arms, the local hotel and bar, formerly a salt proprietor's home in the old days. Back in those days, everyone who lived there pretty much knew everyone else on the Island, especially pilots. Somehow, he ended up tagging along with me in the same Twin Bonanza that I mentioned earlier. On my first takeoff from Grand Turk with him aboard, we were going down the runway at about 50 knots (57 mph), when suddenly a donkey wandered across the airstrip, and I realized that I was going too fast to stop. Disaster awaited with a major aviation personality as my passenger!

Although my speed was increasing, I avoided panic and quickly pulled the stick back, then pushed the stick forward, then pulled it back again and bounced the plane down on the resilient nose gear, then pulled it up quickly in an attempt to bounce the plane up and off the ground. It worked, thanks to the shock absorbers in each wheel. Becoming airborne, I managed to stagger over the top of the donkey and back down the runway, and in about another 100 feet we took off. Looking over at Max, I noticed that his face was white and he wasn't moving, speaking or breathing! "What's the matter, Max?" I muttered, "Don't you ever do that up in Washington?" He muttered, "Jesus H. Christ, I've never seen anything like that in my life!" My keen response was, "Well, with any luck, we won't have to do it again today." And so we just flew on.

To tell the truth, jumping that donkey kind of scared me, too, but I wasn't about to let on. As it turned out, my heroics went unnoticed by the flying public because Max never wrote the story—he believed that it would give the wrong impression about the nature of flying in the West Indies. Safety and reliability took a serious hit the day we jumped the donkey.

During Max's visits, he became fascinated with my wife Noreen, about whom I'll talk more in the next chapter, and he especially loved her Irish brogue. Once, just prior to a scheduled trip the Ireland, he asked her for a traditional Irish saying with which he could greet people. "Póg mo thóin," she replied, and she worked with him until he pronounced that phrase correctly. Needless to say, upon his return a year later, Max chided her for teaching him to say, "Kiss my ass" to the Irish customs inspectors at the airport. It was all good-natured fun, and I'm sure the Irish were used to it.

During my time in the Islands, I avoided having to deliver a baby—but just barely. In 1968, I got a call to fly a pregnant woman from Providenciales to Grand Turk. There were no doctors in Provo at that time, and the poor woman had been in labor for a day and a half. The attending nurse had run out of confidence and thought the woman needed a doctor's help. So, I flew my Cessna 180 4-seater from South Caicos to pick them up.

Imagine my surprise when, after getting the patient situated in my plane, the nurse simply stated, "Well, I have to go back home, now." She was not going to accompany us!

It was getting dark outside, there were no lights on the runway, the woman was in agony in the backseat, so I decided to take off and make the flight. She was moaning and groaning, and I was patting her gently with my right hand while flying with my left.

The she spread her legs, and I immediately believed that she was going to deliver the baby. "A bad idea," I thought. But it was a false alarm.

Getting on the radio, I may have sounded a bit panicky as I called the USAF Base to advise them to phone the hospital to have a vehicle ready and waiting to speed my suffering passenger to the doctor's office. The tower operator joked, "Em, you sure know how to pick 'em, don't you!"

Everything turned out OK, although they told me that she almost had the baby in the car. Mother and child made it, without my medical assistance. For that, I was extremely grateful.

On another occasion, I had been chartered to pick up a passenger at the small village of Kew, an inland farming village in the middle of nothing in North Caicos. I flew over a few times to let the passenger know I was there, then landed and waited for them to walk the half-mile or so out to the plane. While hanging out there, two local female field workers approached me and asked me to give them a ride, for entertainment. "We'll rock on the ground with you, Cap'n Embry," they said. "No thanks," I replied. Although I had been paid by lobsters and fish, I was not going to barter for *that*!

That story brought to mind another flight I made to Kew, this time with some passengers that included a local bishop of the Church of God of Prophecy, a Holiness Pentecostal Christian religion that was big in the Islands. It was pouring rain quite heavily when I flew Bishop Wynns and his congregants there, and therein lay the problem.

There was no airstrip at Kew—we usually landed in a field that had been cleared, but all the grass and vegetation was quite slippery when wet. "It's too drenched—I can't land," I said to the Bishop, as we circled in my twin-engine Piper Aztec. He replied, "Go on, the Lord will take care of us, Embry."

Well, with that inspiration, I gave it a shot. It was like landing on grease—as we skidded and spun around, I gave it the right-engine-left-rudder treatment—more about that move in a later chapter. We finally came to a stop, unscathed. As they all got out and went on their way, Bishop Wynns observed, "I knowed that the Lord was watching over us, Embry." And He surely was that day.

Landing at Kew was also a distressing memory for longtime local politician and leader Hilly Arthur Ewing. Years later, he said, "I can remember when we used to fly that one-engine plane to Grand Turk to council meetings. On our way down, we had to stop for Mr. Robinson and land on the salina in Kew on the back of the village. That used to be the frightful part of flying—wondering how we would get back up in the air."

Hilly's son became a physician, and eventually achieved the position of Chief Minister of the Islands.

An early learning experience occurred on October 10, 1968, when I was flying solo in the Twin Bonanza from Grand Turk to Provo to meet Fritz and the guys.

In the middle of the flight, the temperature started climbing and the oil pressure started dropping on the right engine. Hoping I wasn't going to have an engine failure—because up till then I had only practiced such emergencies, never experiencing the real thing—I was closely monitoring the instruments and the increasing pressure. Finally, the engine made a bunch of horrible, clunky noises and sounded like it was going to shake itself to death. I thought, "I better stop this," so I feathered the engine. Even so, there was still a lot of rattling going on in the right engine, and I could see oil pouring out of it. Never a good sign in an aircraft. I should have feathered the engine sooner.

In a propeller-driven aircraft, feathering an engine means that when an engine fails, in order to decrease drag so you can either glide farther or increase performance on the remaining engine(s), you set the prop pitch lever; so, instead of facing at a right angle to drive air backwards and produce thrust, the propeller instead turns edge-first into the airstream, reducing drag. In other words, the feathering position turns the prop so that the edge faces into the airstream. It's a useful safety feature in many, but not all, propeller-driven planes.

On the other hand, unless you wanted to be dead fast, it was necessary to disable the correct—dead—engine, *not* the functioning one. We pilots had a saying that reminded us what to do in an emergency loss-of-engine crisis: "Dead foot—dead engine." In layman's terms, if the left engine quit, then the left rudder pedal—which helps control the plane—would also be dead. Therefore, a pilot would have to over-steer with the right pedal in order to keep the plane in a straight line. For a pilot to panic in such a situation may cause the plane to start spiraling downward, which is life-threatening.

Anyway, when I finally reached Providenciales, everyone on the ground noticed that the engine was feathered and, with great excitement, they hustled to the plane as I pulled off the runway. We then determined that a couple of cylinders had come off during the flight, and the pistons had literally beat themselves to death—meaning that I had totally ruined the engine. Unfortunate and expensive.

The lesson that I learned was that as soon as I detected the drop in oil pressure and the rise in temperature, I should have feathered it immediately. However, since it was my very first time in such an emergency situation, nobody was too pissed off at me about it. Later, upon reflection, I realized that I had really flown the Twin Bonanza with only one engine. That aspect of this adrenalizing situation provided me with a lot more confidence in both the airplane and my own flying abilities.

Chapter 6: Noreen

It's precisely at this point in my island story that love enters the picture.

I had become very friendly with the Islands' Chief Magistrate, Finbar F. Dempsey. An Irishman, he and his wife Ann had lived there since their arrival in 1964. Finbar and I ran into each other on the street in Grand Turk one day in December 1967, and he casually mentioned that his sister-in-law was coming to town soon, and maybe I'd like to come over to his place and meet her. Not having seen any girls in quite a while, I decided to take him up on his kind suggestion.

Anyway, Finbar was having a party, and, as usual, I just whizzed over there in the Twin Bonanza, parked it and walked up the road to his house. As long as I live, I will never forget the moment that I walked into his kitchen and spied this beautiful girl in a yellow bikini, making sweet and sour pork. That was my future wife, Noreen Theresa Smythe, from Dublin, Ireland. Born in Limerick and raised in Ennis, County Clare, she was quite an attractive, original Irish lass. I'll tell you a lot more about her as this story goes on.

Eventually that evening we went to a big party nearby and had a great time together. At the end of the social gathering, when I asked if she'd like to go out with me again the next day, she said, "Sure." I guess she thought at first that it was pretty cool just to be able to walk down to the airfield, hop in a plane with some fellow and roar off to our next destination. Because that's exactly what we did.

On a later flight, we flew over to South Caicos and I introduced her to Lew. Then we jumped on my Honda, picked up a picnic lunch from somewhere and proceeded to a pleasant, deserted beach on the east coast of the Island. We were picnicking there and having an enjoyable time when suddenly this horrendous noise materialized from the sky. It was Lew—he had taken off, snuck his plane around the edge of the Island, revved it up to about 180 miles per hour over the water and then ripped across the beach at about 5 feet over our heads! I could almost hear him laughing over the engines.

Anyway, Noreen and I were very quickly developing a good relationship. However, on the following day she had a date that she had previously made with another guy; that somewhat annoyed me. While stewing about this predicament, it dawned on me that I could pull Lew's trick on them since I knew they were taking out Finbar's boat, a 16-foot fiberglass job with a Mercury 50hp engine.

So, I was in the middle of a scheduled run from Grand Turk to Salt Cay, when I spied their boat in the sea about three miles away. After I finished my business at Salt Cay, I took off, skimmed exceptionally low over the water and approached them from behind at a high rate of speed. However, they had the boat's engine revving, and at first it appeared that they didn't hear me because I was too low on the water. Flying over them as fast as I could manage, I changed the pitch of the propellers, making quite a horrendous racket; then, I shot straight up and returned to Grand Turk.

Later, I discovered that what I thought was such a funny trick had actually caused great consternation—Noreen's sister thought that the boat was blowing up, and she always alleged that she threw young baby Paul overboard to save him. Needless to say, I was rather unpopular in the Dempsey household for a time due to this almost-disastrous stunt. It must not have negatively affected young Paul Dempsey since he eventually became a very prominent and respectable lawyer in the Islands. In fact, Dempsey and Company remains today the longest established legal practice in the Turks and Caicos.

One thing led to another in the relationship between Noreen and me, and I eventually told her that I loved her and wanted to marry. She, in turn, thought that I was a typical Yank: a bit stupid with a burning desire to do everything immediately. However, the good news is that when she returned to Eleuthera in the Bahamas, where her English fiancée was a banker, she informed him that she was ending their engagement. I thought that was a very compelling positive sign for me since he was next in line for an English Lordship—and she would have been "Lady Noreen" had they married.

Time went on, and we ended up rendezvousing in both New York and Puerto Rico. Noreen worked as a hostess for Aer Lingus, the flag carrier airline of Ireland. Once, she had a two-day layover in New York City, and I took a commercial flight out of Nassau to meet her. In fact, we saw Dustin Hoffman's hit movie *The Graduate* during our time together. At that time in our lives, it just seemed like no big deal to fly to New York for a couple of days to connect with someone you really liked.

Noreen and I wanted to rendezvous again a few weeks later but had difficulty making a plan. We had to cable each other and use our radio telephone lines—remember that there weren't any answering machines or cell phones at that time. We preferred to go skiing together in Austria, but the plans would just not work, so we met instead in Puerto Rico. Noreen could access a free flight there on one of the numerous Caribbean International Airways (CIA!) operations that existed during that era.

As a result, we met in San Juan; however, I couldn't find any vacant hotel rooms because it was Washington's Birthday, and it seemed like every New Yorker had flown to Puerto Rico for a long weekend getaway. Luckily, at the airport, I met someone who knew somebody who could put us up for a few days. Our rescuer turned out to be a German or Austrian woman in her 60s who had formerly been the riding instructor for the Trujillo family and children in the Dominican Republic. Rafael Trujillo had ruled the DR with an iron hand as dictator from 1930 to 1961. This very interesting lady allowed us to stay at her dwelling for several days.

Noreen and I had a fine time on that trip. One day, we travelled to St. Thomas in the nearby U.S. Virgin Islands to visit some friends from Louisville—Britt Bryant and Peyton Gresham. Britt worked as a lawyer in the Virgins Islands, and Peyton, his wife, was a distant cousin of mine. Britt and Peyton still live in the Virgin Islands—although now in St. Croix.

We always enjoyed visiting Santo Domingo, the capital of the Dominican Republic. One of the Caribbean's oldest cities, it was founded in 1496 by Bartholomew Columbus, younger brother of Christopher. We enjoyed touring one of the period museums located there, and we were constantly amazed that the sleeping beds and suits of armor appeared to have been made for a people far, far shorter than we were.

Following a suggestion by our friend Jim Hodge, Noreen and I once went to Constanza, located about 4,000 feet up in the central mountain range of the DR. You'll learn more about Jim and his connections in the next chapter. That area in the DR is noted for its remarkable mountain climate, despite being on a tropical island. We stayed in an almost-empty hotel that had been built by the regime of DR strongman Trujillo.

That trip was always memorable to me because of the horses we rented. Actually, they were just short ponies. We were riding them through an area that was being farmed by garlic-growers when my mount bent its neck around in an acrobatic move and bit my leg. Noreen heard me say, "It's biting me!" and replied, "Don't be silly." Then it bit me again. Hard. We cut that trip short.

On another journey to Santo Domingo, Noreen and I stayed at Jim Hodge's house; he was always very accommodating. We always hung out at the InterContinental Hotel there. During our stay, we received a phone call from Jim, in New York, who frantically wanted to know if we were OK due to the report he had received of riots and shootings in downtown Santo Domingo. This was an example of the gross exaggeration of news reports that regularly emanated from the Caribbean and West Indies in that era. We were alright, and so was Santo Domingo. We all survived.

Not long after that, by communicating via radio telephone through a ham radio operator in Alexandra, Virginia, I informed my parents that I was in love with a wonderful woman whom I wished to marry; and, if they wanted to meet her, they should take an opportunity to come down to Grand Turk. It all happened as arranged. My parents visited me in the Islands, and Noreen returned to Grand Turk. Everybody met each other, they all approved and the marriage was on!

Officially, our engagement was announced on May 16, 1968 in the *Courier-Journal* as follows: "Mr. and Mrs. Timothy Fannan (sic) Smythe of Ennis, County Clare, Ireland, announce the engagement of their daughter, Miss Noreen Theresa Smythe, to Mr. Embry Cobb Rucker, Jr., of South Caicos, British West Indies, son of the Rev. and Mrs. Embry Cobb Rucker of Alexandria, Va., formerly of Louisville." Note that my future father-in-law's name was misspelled—it should have read "Flannan."

Noreen was a very bright and intelligent woman. So much so that she skipped a couple of years in school—much to the irritation of her sister, who was often reminded of that fact.

When she was a teenager, Noreen had an interesting German connection. At age 17, she was hired by a German family to teach English to their children and to serve as kind of a Mummy's helper. Her German family went to

Istanbul, Turkey for six or seven months, and Noreen travelled with them. Quite an adventure. Plus, the job also allowed her to learn German.

It paid off. When she eventually returned to Ireland, she was hired by a German-owned manufacturing company to work as a translator at Shannon Airport in County Clare. I'm sure her ability to speak a couple of languages helped her land the job as a stewardess for Aer Lingus. Strange as it may seem, at that time, being a stewardess was considered one of the best jobs for a woman in Ireland. Her airline treated stewardesses royally at all their destinations, including special vans to transport them to their hotels.

Noreen's father, Tim Smythe, was a Clare county councilor—a local government elected official—from 1950 to 1974, and a noted international cross-country champion. The Fairgreen, a space that hosts fairs, in Ennis is named after him. She had three brothers: Barry, Mike and Conor; and four sisters: Maeve, Maura, Ann and Olive. Quite a nice family. My father-in law's name opened many doors for me in Ireland. Whenever I was out in the countryside or city without Noreen at my side, I only had to casually mention, "I am married to Tim Smythe's daughter," for strangers to take notice and become more friendly and helpful. Not that they weren't already, but I always got an extra boost of assistance when they knew we were kin.

The next time that we all met together was in July 1968 when Mother and I travelled to Ireland for my wedding. My father couldn't attend because it was a really busy time for him, and I was alright with that. He told me that he could either go to Ireland or contribute funds for our expenses, and I told him, "It's up to you." My brother Rudy, who had married Sylvia the previous year, also couldn't attend due to his schedule and the cost that was involved. A few of my German cousins were present on my behalf, in addition to 250 of Noreen's closest friends and relations.

The pre-wedding plane flight I took to Ireland was interesting. Needless to say, the crew on our Aer Lingus flight had been alerted that Noreen's fellow was on board, and they proceeded to get me drunk as a hoot owl. Upon arrival, I didn't make a very good impression on Noreen's family. Her dad, a real outdoorsman and athlete, had never had a drink in his life. For him to see his prospective son-in-law coming off the plane half drunk at 8:00 in the morning was not one of my most successful or memorable moments. However, her parents and I ended up getting along very well and having a very enjoyable relationship.

Fortunately, I relied upon my Mother to keep me straightened out and to tell me what to do during the wedding and all the events leading up to it. So, Noreen and I became husband and wife, and then we spent a wonderful honeymoon travelling all over Ireland, starting at Ennis, the county town of County Clare.

Eventually, all that fun ended, and we went back to the Islands. My logbook entry on August 13, 1968 indicates that I flew from Miami to South Caicos "with new wife." Of course, upon returning to the Islands, I realized that I hadn't made any arrangements for a place to live, which was really stupid, no matter how you look at it. For a time, we lived in a hotel room at the Admiral's Arms. Then Lew announced that he was going to be gone for a week or two, destination unknown, and that we could stay in the Caicos Airways house. What a relief.

Upon Lew's departure, I flew each and every day, seven days a week, dawn to dusk, to cover the entire schedule while he was gone. Lew was in Turks and Caicos for less than a year, and he was actually gone a good bit of that time.

Well, the second week sped by and Lew still hadn't returned. Ditto the third week. And the fourth. After seven weeks, Lew still had not appeared, no one had any idea where he was and I continued to fly the schedule every day of the week, from 7:00 in the morning until dark, with no relief. Perhaps Noreen was beginning to think that she had married a lunatic with whom she was stuck on this little island.

Meanwhile, she was making friends and getting to know everyone on the island. She even started a garden, which was unheard of in South Caicos. One day, a local guy came to the airport and spoke to me, saying, "Cap'n Embry, Cap'n Embry. Your wife sick, Man, the sun got her in the head." I quickly replied, "Why's that?" The man responded, "Man, Ms. Embry she goin' around with this basket pickin' up all the donkey dirt." Well, I realized right away that Noreen was trying to make soil for her vegetable garden, and she was just gathering up manure here and there. The old, wild donkeys that roamed the islands left it all over the island roads, so it seemed to her to be a perfectly logical part of her gardening. However, the local people thought she was right out of her tree.

Not long after I met Noreen, I had gone to Fritz Ludington and told him that I wanted to get married. He reacted by saying, "Well, me and Tommy'd have to talk about it." After a while they called me and declared, "Well, we talked about it and decided that you can get married." Then they just burst out laughing—they thought that was the funniest thing. At that time, they were still only paying me $300 a month salary plus expenses. Later, they said they would give me a raise—my pay was being increased to $1,000 a month, plus I could live in the Caicos house rent-free. This was just like a bolt out of the blue! A thousand dollars a month was plenty of money for us, plus a place to live—this, even after Lew returned, if he ever did.

The South Caicos house in question was a two-story structure, sort of run-down, with a metal roof and shingles on the exterior. It had an open kitchen with running water and a kerosene refrigerator, but no stove. To solve that deficiency, we made frequent use of our hot plate, and we would grill outside sometimes; eventually, we purchased a little box oven. The second floor was all open space. We kept a few spare beds available upstairs for visitors from Provo or Provident who dropped in. All in all, we liked it very much.

At long last Lew did emerge from wherever it was he went, and I had some relief from the daily flying duties. That's when Noreen and I decided to make up for some lost time by having a picnic.

We chose to go to East Caicos, a deserted island about 20 miles long, and we travelled in the Cessna 180 that I mentioned earlier. At that time, East Caicos Island had seen no inhabitants for about 80 years. We had to land in a salina—a salt-lake or marsh that is too low for anything to grow on, but just high enough to be dry. As we landed there, it dawned on me that this would be just the romantic bee's knees: the entire day to picnic on a deserted island with an attractive woman and a beautiful beach.

Leaving the airplane, we walked over to the beach, took off all our clothes, started swimming and having a great time. Then, all of a sudden, we noticed the mosquitoes. Then, more and more mosquitoes. Their numbers reached the point where Noreen and I had to stay submerged with our noses barely out of the water, just to be able to breathe and to escape the swarming mosquitoes. Finally, we decided that the only way out of this mess was to make a mad dash for the plane. So, racing naked out of the water, we snatched our clothes off the beach, ran through a couple hundred feet of bush, jumped frantically into the airplane and rapidly took off. We didn't even bother to close the doors—as we gained altitude, the wind eventually blew all the mosquitoes out of the airplane. There we were, both stark naked, with the doors of the airplane open, flying through the air with the greatest of ease. Looking at each other, we immediately started laughing uproariously! Needless to say, we managed to get some clothes on before we returned to the airport at South Caicos.

Later, we heard some scary stories about cows actually being suffocated by similar swarms of mosquitoes which would clog the poor beast's air passages. Evidently, the locals acquired some immunity to the gnats and sandflies in the Islands, and mosquitoes were really no problem— unless you were in East Caicos. Many years later, when I asked my friend Florita Gibbs of Lorimers how she kept the mosquitoes away, she replied, "By making smoke with all kinds of things, peas' shuck…and cow dung. That's how we used to get relief from the mosquitoes. After we got electricity, we used the coil, Off and Flit to keep them away."

Not all our good times were so harried. On another more successful picnic, we took a small 15-foot skiff and went up to Nigger Cay, a small island near South Caicos. When I first arrived in the islands, I was sensitive about using the name Nigger Cay. In fact, not being comfortable with the use of the "N" word, I used to refer to it as, "Oh, yeah, that little island up there." However, I realized that all the local people referred to it quite openly as Nigger Cay and it didn't seem to bother them. Then I saw that all the Turks and Caicos Island maps listed Nigger Cay as an official island name, so I didn't see any sense in worrying about it. Anyway, we had a nice trip there. Puttering up the coast, we found little Nigger Cay, had our picnic on the deserted island, did some fishing and then returned. Another day in paradise.

Noreen didn't do much scuba diving, but I certainly enjoyed it. I even acquired an underwater camera. It was fun to see turtles, sting rays and other sea life up close— but not sharks. Once, off the east coast of South Caicos, I was diving when I noticed everyone in the boat waving frantically at me. That was when I realized that five or six sharks were swimming back and forth under me. Discretion being the better part of valor, as they say, I swam to the safety of the boat as quickly as possible.

Near Salt Cay, and at Big Sand Cay, I would see a great many nurse sharks, common inshore bottom-dwelling sharks found in tropical waters; it was a popular place for them to breed and give birth to their young. These sharks would grow up to about 10 feet in length.

There is a reef about 10 miles south of Big Sand Cay where the wreckage of the oldest British warship in the Americas can be found—HMS *Endymion*. With the top of the reef only 4-5 feet below the water, it's an interesting location: just a reef with the full sea running over it, and no place to anchor. The wreck itself is only about 40 feet under water.

There were four ships in the Royal Navy named after the Greek hero Endymion. This one was built in 1779 and was a 44-gun large frigate which went down in 1790. After striking the reef, it floundered for three days before sinking; all the crew survived. The site where the ship wrecked is known as Endymion Rock. Today, the cannons, anchors and chains are the main recognizable remaining features of the wreck.

There are three other wrecks on top of the *Endymion*, including the *General Pershing*, a five-masted schooner with a very early diesel engine, which wrecked on the same rock in 1921. The area surrounding the HMS *Endymion* is a protected historical site; therefore, it is illegal to remove or damage any historical artifact there. However, there really isn't anyone in the area policing this prohibition.

When I made my first descent at that reef, I was with my diving buddies—some Canadian guys and others—on a boat that we took out from Grand Turk. The circumstances definitely made it an unusual dive for me. The sea conditions were rough and surging; our boat was pitching about a lot. Upon surfacing and climbing back on the ship, I became extremely seasick—which seldom occurred. And I was stupid enough to return and dive there again a couple of years later.

My brother Rudy made an eventful visit to the Islands in 1969. He had never scuba dived before, so I arranged for us to go out with Paul Hudson, the local dive-master. The plan was to give Rudy the typical quickie resort-course training session, closely supervised. It didn't quite work out that way.

Paul and I had instructed Rudy about the dangers involved in diving, such as malfunctioning equipment, pulmonary embolism and the bends; we emphasized that he should breathe out when going up and to follow his bubbles.

Well, he and I went down to our desired depth, but Rudy wanted to go deeper. And deeper. We went to an amazing 200 feet, but I was more concerned about the fact that we were near the place that the ocean floor fell to 7,000 feet. Then, Rudy started acting funny, and I eventually almost had to drag him up to the surface. It was a scary moment for me with my brother.

My concern was that he was developing nitrogen narcosis, a condition in which his judgment and senses were impaired, almost like being high. A lot of new divers succumb to that danger.

Upon surfacing, I told Paul what happened, and he became upset. When Rudy blew his nose, it was bloody and Rudy asked what was happening. Pau replied, "It's an air embolism, and you're going to die!" Upon hearing that, Rudy became extremely upset until we convinced him that Paul was making a bad joke.

Many years later, I ran into Paul in Provo and mentioned to him that his dive-master persona had been incorporated into one of the fictional characters in a book that Rudy had written. I promised to send him a copy, but I warned, "You don't look so great in it, Paul." Rudy remembered.

Among the Island locals, one of my good friends was an entrepreneur named Noel Ewing from the town of Kew on North Caicos. Noel had worked in Georgia and Mississippi picking cotton and he had a lot of stories about what it was like to be black in the USA's deep South in those days. He loved to BS and was an exceptional storyteller.

Born in 1932, Noel remembered, "I saw the first plane fly over and it scared everybody to death—everybody headed for the bushes." He continued, "I bought the first car, a Cadillac. I bought it in the states. You had to ship via Provo." He ended up in Kew and owned and operated a small bar there. "I held the first bar license on the Island in 1962," he declared in a later interview. "This was the first place you were able to sit down and have a drink, or smoke and dance. I also had two juke boxes. We didn't have too many accidents in those days—donkey was our main transportation."

Kew was the only non-waterfront village in the Turks and Caicos, and one of its sections was known to locals as Scandalous Corner. It was just someplace different to go drinking and probably had done nothing to earn its name; however, that's what it was called.

Noel had more memories of that bar he owned: "People used to buy the monkey bag drink—that used to sell more than anything else, and people used to like to get drunk. They would come and get drunk and then go home speaking in tongues. Their children couldn't even understand it, mam would go in the corner. We used to get the monkey bag from Haiti in barrels." As much as I can tell, monkey bag was some kind of demon rum that was imported—or, most likely, smuggled—from Haiti.

My friend Noel was also responsible for bringing the first truck to Kew, using a freighter-sailboat to do so. Then, to build a route to reach the town, he engaged several women to chop a roadway with their machetes. At one point, he turned on the vehicle's wiper blades and headlights to clear the windshield of debris and to see through the rain, and one of the women loudly proclaimed, "Lawd, look at that—it wipe it own face, and fire come out of the mouth!" They had never seen a motor vehicle before. "When they saw the lights, they started jumping over the walls—that was the beginning of the motor vehicle in North Caicos," said Noel. "Before that they used donkey, and some of the donkeys died on the way. So I was pretty famous."

On one memorable occasion, I was flying the Governor of the Bahamas, the Governor of the Turks and Caicos and several other English administrators on a goodwill tour of the Islands. When we landed at the airport in North Caicos, all the local dignitaries were lined up to meet the esteemed visitors, and there was Noel—uninvited—lined up with them!

One of the largest local industries in the Islands was the lobster processing plant on South Caicos. These warm-water, Caribbean spiny lobsters—*panularus argus*, I believe—have no claws; however, their large tails are filled with meat. The Turks Islander locals capture them by free-diving, with no scuba equipment, and by snaring them one at a time with a bully stick. Eventually, the lobster tail is wrung—or twisted—off and stored frozen in the nearby processing plant until being sent to Miami.

Divers were a big deal when I was lived in the Islands. They had money and boats, and they were manly men. That has changed over time. In my 2005 interview with her, my friend Lynette Mills Bassett observed, "Years ago, 600-800 pounds of lobster was nothing for them to free dive. (Today) the young people are not interested in diving." Despite that remark, lobster and conch still remain the Islands' chief exports; in fact, the world's first commercial conch farm was started on Providenciales.

There was a place on the waterfront that I regularly visited along with a lot of local divers—Lloyd Stubbs Topless Bar. Before you get the wrong idea, it was called that because it had just four walls and no roof!

Fish has always been the main food staple in the Islands, not so much meat. In the early 1970s, there was a once-a-week flight from Miami that brought in fresh meat, but no other foodstuffs. My friend George Nipanich once informed me, "Embry, you know that meat that comes in from Haiti? It's horsemeat—you can tell from the deep red color." Of course, the Haitians didn't mind eating it; to them, meat was meat.

Now for a morality tale. There was an older American I used to chat with who lived in South Caicos. Maybe he wasn't as aged as he seemed; although he appeared to be 85, he could have been 55 for all I know. This gentleman, who was called Uncle Richie, had come to the islands around 15 years earlier to work as a handyman and mechanic maintaining the generators and freezers for the local lobster fisheries, and he just decided to stay. As my friend Bill Clare from South Caicos recalled, "…we had a white person running the plant (Caicos Fisheries) and who was the mechanic—we just had a few." Uncle Richie lived with a very nice local woman named Cully—we used to buy bread from her. He managed to do his job and lived a nice, quiet life, but was perhaps too fond of the bottle.

I got to know Uncle Richie pretty well. One day he stopped me on the street and our conversation went like this:

Uncle Richie: "Hey, Boy!"

Me: "Yeah, Uncle Richie, what up?"

Richie: "You like it here, eh?"

Me: "Oh yeah, I like it here fine—I'm having a great time. I'm always running around, flying airplanes, going to the beach, enjoying the beautiful tropical weather and being a big cheese in a small pond."

Richie: "Well, you want to watch it. If you stay here too long, your brain shrinks up to about the size of a pea, and you can't live nowhere else. That's what happened to me."

At the time, I laughed at what my friend said; but, after I had lived there for several years, I began to see the truth in his remarks. Indeed, I saw this condition affect people who settled in the Islands from the States. They stayed there until they literally couldn't function anywhere else, for whatever reason. Luckily, Noreen and I avoided that sad fate.

Another note about Lew Whinnery: After a very brief stay back in the Islands, he just disappeared again, which he had a habit of doing. I didn't see him for a long time, but I heard a rumor that he was in Puerto Rico. Long after that, in the 1970s, when I was flying fruits and vegetables out of San Juan, I asked around at the airport to determine if anyone knew him. Someone claimed to, and gave me his phone number. In a short time, I called the number, and sure enough, there's Lew on the other end. He had married some girl, and they were living in Puerto Rico where Lew was the head of maintenance and flying for some local air service outfit, Prinair or maybe Caribbean International. Once I knew he was there, I started seeing quite a bit of him—he helped us get out of some messy scrapes in San Juan. As far as legalities were concerned, many of our flying habits and licensing certifications were questionable, especially in U.S. territories such as Puerto Rico.

On another mini-vacation around 1974 or '75, Noreen and I travelled to Belize City where we had reserved a room in a nice lodge; then, we journeyed to the mountains in Guatemala to view Tikal, the ruins of an ancient city found in a rainforest and some other well-known Mayan temples.

That was quite an excursion. When we arrived at the border between Belize, which used to be British Honduras, and Guatemala, Noreen had only her Irish passport, which the Guatemalans wouldn't recognize. The border officials indicated that she needed a visa to access Guatemala. I was deemed okay to enter because I possessed an American passport.

Eventually, after our lodge owner negotiated intensely with them, they allowed Noreen entry into their country, but only after we agreed that she would leave her passport on the Belize side, since then she would still technically be in Belize and not in Guatemala. Go figure. More frightening, shortly after that, a truckload of teen-aged Guatemalan military servicemen passed by with their guns pointed right at us. Not a comfortable feeling.

When we finally reached Tikal, it was fantastically beautiful. We climbed up innumerable steps to reach the summit of the temple, but we had trouble descending, because Noreen's agoraphobia reared up. She just froze and couldn't move. Eventually, after slowly traversing sideways down the steps, her condition suddenly moderated and we made it back okay.

Noreen's agoraphobia had struck once earlier when we were tourists at an icon of Haiti's history. We were showing some visitors from Hughes AirWest company the famous fortress from the early 1800s called The Citadelle, located on the northern coast near Cap-Haïtien, and one of the most popular tourist destinations in Haiti. This huge fortification was built by Henri Christophe, a former slave who became a Haitian leader, to defend the country from the French.

Visitors must complete the final portion of the journey to The Citadelle, located on a treacherous mountaintop, on horseback or on foot. The entire seven-mile trail is almost completely uphill, and should only be walked by experienced hikers who carry plenty of water. Most of the interior of The Citadelle fortress is accessible to visitors, who must also climb the numerous staircases to the fortress roof, which is free of guardrails.

Noreen made it up there, but couldn't quite make it back due to her anxiety over feeling that she was trapped in that place—agoraphobia. We had to place a jacket over her head and slowly, evenly guide her down in order to return.

Around 1969, I was appointed to the first tourist board that was organized to officially promote the Islands. Fritz, some locals and some ex-pats also served. The main thrust of this effort was to keep the development of the Islands minimal and exclusive, and to promote jobs for the locals, who then numbered about 5,000. I hoped that such a central board would help quiet some of the rivalry that was apparent between South Caicos and Providenciales.

Eventually, Daphne James of Jamaica was hired as the first paid staffer of this tourist board.

At that time, there were only small hotels and the fishing industry in which locals could find steady work. Eventually, our entire exclusivity plan became terribly skewed by some locals who had visions of big money pouring into the Islands from giant hotels and casinos. As so often happens, several unscrupulous developers became involved, the two-story hotels got out of hand and became 3 to 11 stories, and the locals saw none of the big money.

By the way, over the years the cruise lines have impacted the environment much more than the economy, since they've been making the Islands a regular stop. It has been alleged that these mammoth vessels typically discharge their waste products into the local waters, while their departing passengers spend minimal dollars at local shops.

Back to more good news: Noreen and I were blessed with two wonderful children during the early years of our marriage: Siofra Maire, born on December 26, 1970, and Embry III, whose birth date was January 29, 1973.

There's quite a story about Siofra's birth. Noreen and I were riding my Honda motorcycle, going to her sister Ann's place for Christmas dinner and festivities. It was her last month of pregnancy, and Noreen was quite large. As we sped to Ann's, we noticed Dr. Mick Frank going the other way. We waved the good doctor over, and Noreen described to him the pains she had just started experiencing. He surmised that they were labor pains, and he advised going straight to Grand Turk Hospital. "We can't go to the hospital," we explained, "because we're going to Ann Dempsey's for Christmas." He replied, "Then there's a good chance of having the baby at Ann's." So, we reluctantly went to the hospital.

Well, on Christmas Day, Noreen and I greeted a constant stream of visitors who brought all manner of food and drink, without rest. Bonnie Rowley even brought a baby jar filled with brandy, sneaking it into the room in her purse.

Eventually, I returned home that evening—in those times, it wasn't routine for husbands to be present with their wives during baby deliveries. The next morning, I was awakened by Dr. Frank pounding on my door at home to tell me that I was the father of a beautiful baby girl—Siofra!

Another amusing anecdote: Shortly after that, we were renting a house on Middle Street, right next door to a cat house—a house of prostitution—ably managed by a head girl named Valentine, but pronounced "Walentine." Any time that Noreen needed a babysitter for young Siofra, Valentine arranged for one of her girls to jump over the dividing wall and assist us. Oh well, they say it takes a village.

In 1973, thanks to my service on the national Tourism Board, my family and I were featured in a poster advertising "The Turks & Caicos Islands—Hidden Between Miami and Puerto Rico." The photo shows Noreen carrying little Embry on her hip, with Siofra walking between us, holding our hands, as we walk toward the lighthouse on Grand Turk. It's a pretty neat poster, and I am glad I still have a framed copy.

My friend and Legislative Councilman Norman Saunders from South Caicos was very involved with tourism. He recalled, "I got elected in '67, but somewhere around '70-'72…our mission was to tour the Caribbean and check on their development, and make recommendations for the Turks and Caicos Islands on what we should pursue as a national development. We visited the Bahamas, Cayman Islands, Barbados, British Virgin Islands and Martinique…Our recommendation was to develop and pursue Tourism as our goal. The Legislature accepted that report and therefore set up the Tourist Board and the first Tourist Board legislation. The Legislature appointed me as Chairman."

Norman continued, "There was no other tourism established by '67. Shortly after Fritz (Ludington) built the Third Turtle Inn, I remember Embry coming in and bringing Fritz, who spent a lot of time at the Admiral's Arms."

As a member of the Tourism Board, I was once chartered to fly my fellow members to Haiti to examine that country's tourism efforts. That led to a strange discovery. Eight or ten of us were exploring a Haitian mountain that was 8-10,000 feet high, and the local Islanders among us were amazed beyond description at every step we climbed—they were not used to anything so towering, since the highest elevation on Turks and Caicos was about 150 feet! It demonstrated to me how strongly people become acclimated to their familiar surroundings.

Unfortunately, there were also some negative things occurring in the Islands. In the early 1970s, I heard a lot of second-hand talk about drug smuggling. Evidently, the Islands were a convenient spot for drug dealers to stop and refuel their planes, especially because there was minimal law enforcement in the area. Such drug trafficking had become really bad at the time of my departure in 1976. A lot of people became interested in short-term, big money. As my friend Jim Bassett from South Caicos observed, "Our potential faded away after the drugs came along."

Yes, the Islands had certainly become popular for people with a lot of cash. On one St. Patrick's Day, two California men checked into the Admiral's Arms; they said they were there to investigate starting a fishery. Inquiring where to go for a good time, they were directed to the huge party that Noreen and I were throwing on that great Irish feast day. What a celebration—George Nipanich even performed his famous Cossack dance, showing off his squats, jumps and spins. At party's end, one of the California guys opened his briefcase, completely filled with cash, and said, "What do I owe you?" Of course, we declined payment and said we were just glad to have their company. They explained that they had won big money in Las Vegas on the way down to the Islands. A likely story.

The Islands also had a history of wrecker activity. Wreckers were locals who set up false lights to lure ships into areas where they would crash on rocks or reef; the culprits would then loot the ship's cargo. This was typical of a local Island attitude: We are Us, everything else is Them. I believe that same attitude was later applied to the illegal drug trafficking, mentioned above, to which the locals showed a blind eye.

Due to the worsening of local corruption, the British in recent years had to resume tighter control of the Islands. In 2009, the United Kingdom suspended the Turks and Caicos Islands self-government after allegations and proof of ministerial corruption. Home rule was eventually restored in the islands after the 2012 elections. Unfortunately, this governmental chaos has been an historical pattern.

The Turks and Caicos Islands are composed mostly of Crown Land, which is a territorial area belonging to the monarch, who personifies the Crown. It is the equivalent of an entailed estate and passes with the monarchy, being inseparable from it. Crown Land is supposed to be leased only under very stringent terms. However, the Islands became a popular destination for land speculators since there were no property taxes there. A British foreign minister once told me, "Turks and Caicos is the most troublesome of all the British colonies."

Be that as it may, it was also the most wonderful paradise imaginable in which a young couple in love could begin their marriage and raise their children.

Chapter 7: Twin Beeches and DC-3s

Meanwhile, time in the Islands rolled on, giving us many pleasant memories and introducing us to scores of very enjoyable people. Of course, there was always a busy flying schedule to maintain.

Around 1970, we reckoned that we were really moving up in the aviation world when we bought or leased some Beechcraft Model 18 aircraft, or Twin Beeches as they were commonly called. One at a time, they started to arrive; they appealed to us because they increased the number of passengers we could accommodate. These 18Ds were twin-engine, low-wing, tailwheel light aircraft designed and manufactured by the Beech Aircraft Corporation from 1937 to around 1969, although the last models were much different than the originals. They would hold a pilot plus up to 10 passengers, depending on how many seats could be added. Quite a few of the Twin Beeches that I flew were as old as me, similar to the aging DC-3s which I'll discuss later.

During World War II, many Twin Beech 18s were reproduced and reprogrammed as C-45s, AT-11s and SNBs for military use by our armed forces. The Twin Beech 18 can now be found all throughout the world, being used in practically every possible way imaginable. It is still frequently encountered in bush country, where it is flown and loved by backcountry pilots.

As effective as they were, Twin Beeches were a challenge to operate when taxiing on our short Island airstrips; also, when a cross wind came up, they could ground loop terribly. One time I landed at Grand Turk during a very unusual wet season, dropping just over the power lines and touching down. As soon as I touched the brakes, I realized that the rain had made the strip as slick as glass. There was no braking action whatsoever on my plane. So, we just continued to roll along, and then I decided we were going to end up in the cemetery—literally—if I didn't find a solution. So, I hit full left rudder, then full right engine, then spun the plane around. When it had spun halfway around, going in the opposite direction, I reversed the procedure, hitting full right rudder, then full left engine until the plane stopped spinning, whereupon I cut both engines. Of course, our momentum was still carrying us down the landing strip toward the cemetery wall, but instead of rolling forward, we were rolling backward and pointing in the wrong direction. Then I applied the power, and we slowly stopped rolling. It was a spectacular show for my five passengers, who all thought it was great—they didn't know that we weren't supposed to be doing that, and that an unfortunate end might have been in store for them. It was a great trick, and I was lucky to get away with it, at a time when I absolutely needed to. Later, after more practice, I perfected that maneuver and could do it most anywhere if I needed to and the situation called for it, even with the bigger DC-3s.

At that time, Caicos Airways was starting to branch out by flying to a variety of destinations, and I was putting a lot of hours in operating Twin Beeches. We were running passenger charters to: Haiti; Santo Domingo in the Dominican Republic, always a favorite with single fellows because of the nightlife and attractive women; Puerto Rico; Kingston, Jamaica; and, as always, Nassau and Florida.

A very organized gentleman from South Caicos named Mills was our first Agent for Caicos Airways. He was a very bright guy. His daughter, Lynette Mills Bassett, remembered her father with these words: "My father was a very intelligent man…District Commissioner Ewing mentored him...he had a knack for management...he was always business-like." Her husband, my good friend Jim Bassett, worked to maintain the Pan Am radio beacon on South Caicos that was so important in helping aircraft to stay on course in that part of the world. Jim was an interesting character. In addition to being an enthusiastic ham radio operator, he was always interested in airplanes. He eventually developed an American accent just by listening to the broadcasts!

Our next major move was acquiring Douglas DC-3s. Those were big, serious fixed-wing, propeller-driven airplanes. They had a range of 1,500 miles, could cruise at 150 mph and carried up to 30 passengers, in comfort. Introduced in 1936, the DC-3 revolutionized air transport for that era. Its lasting effect on the airline industry and World War II made it one of the most significant transport aircraft ever made.

In order to acquire my air transport pilot's license, I returned to the States in 1970 and used the GI Bill to train to fly DC-3s. Pregnant at the time, Noreen accompanied me; Siofra would be born on December 26. The term GI Bill refers to benefits earned by veterans after leaving active duty. Starting after World War II, the GI Bill was designed to help service members and eligible veterans cover the costs associated with getting an education or training. And that I did.

Returning to the Islands, I flew co-pilot for a short while, then captained DC-3s on regularly scheduled flights. They handled great, but most importantly for us, they were reliable, easy to maintain and could operate from short runways.

In fact, although we were using the same short airstrips, we kept leasing or buying larger airplanes. At one point, I landed a DC-3 on the downtown airstrip with about 45 people on board. Luckily, we weren't carrying any baggage and we were light on fuel; however, that was still somewhat pushing the safety factor.

A few years ago, my sister-in-law Maeve Smythe sent me a photo taken in November 1970, showing me in the middle of about a dozen people around a DC-3. Countess Helen Czernin is sitting on a block under the left wing, tall Billy Joe Dodson, our heavy equipment operator, is looking at the photographer, and Gustav Lightbourne, the local representative to the legislative assembly, is the black gentleman with arms akimbo. Quite a group. The plane appears to be filled with lumber. The basketball and sports complex on Providenciales was later named after Gustav.

In 1971, the British government finally decided to use its influence to persuade the authorities at the United States Air Force Base, located approximately one mile from the downtown airstrip, to grant us permission to land there. Success! Much better than landing on Church Folly Street.

Over the years, the United States operated several military installations on the Turks and Caicos. From 1959 to 1980, there was a U.S. Coast Guard facility on South Caicos that ran a LORAN Navigation station, which functioned similar to a global, radar-based GPS system for ship and aircraft navigation. LORAN stood for LOng Range Aid to Navigation.

From 1954 to 1979, on the north end of Grand Turk was a U.S. Navy facility called North Base, a spy-type operation staffed by a few officers and a couple hundred sailors, which monitored Soviet submarine activity with an underwater listening system. South Base was a U.S. Air Force satellite-tracking facility on Grand Turk with one USAF officer and many civilians working for Pan American Airways & RCA. This operation was part of the eastern missile tracking range which tracked all the rockets launched by NASA from Cape Kennedy—formerly Cape Canaveral. The USAF used the runway once or twice a week for supply flights, and U.S. Navy planes also landed there.

The United States also constructed an airstrip on South Caicos for the military during World War II.

Norman Saunders from South Caicos recalled, "The Americans built a base here prior to 1943. At that time, they had no interaction or influence with the community..."

South Base is where astronaut Colonel John Glenn first touched shore shortly after his three orbits of earth in 1962, one of the most famous flights in the history of U.S. aviation. His Mercury space capsule, named *Friendship* 7, splashed down in the Atlantic Ocean east of the Turks and Caicos, and a Navy destroyer picked him up and delivered him to Grand Turk before his return stateside. Another destroyer picked up the capsule itself and delivered it to Grand Turk where it was loaded aboard a USAF plane at the airport and eventually returned to Florida. Glenn was taken to Cockburn Town on Grand Turk for several days for medical checkups and debriefing. The 2016 movie *Hidden Figures* detailed this flight, but without mentioning Turks and Caicos. Of course, that all occurred before I arrived in the Islands.

Today, there is a replica of the *Friendship* 7 space capsule outside the JAGS McCartney International Airport on Grand Turk, just south of Cockburn Town. James Alexander George Smith McCartney (1945-1980) was the Territory's first Chief Minister and first National Hero.

Former Legislative Council member Gustavus Lightbourne accurately observed, "If it hadn't been for the two Bases, Grand Turk would have become sleeping—the reason Grand Turk began climbing out of this state was because of the Bases." Prominent local Oswaldo Ariza recalled, "Two Army companies built the Bases, and they built the Air Force Base in 1952. This was all in connection with the missile program." Oswaldo, an electrician and amateur historian, was a very good friend of mine. In fact, he and his brother Juan—which all the locals pronounced Wong—did the wiring for the first house that I built on Grand Turk in the early 1970s.

Regarding space exploration, Grand Turk played an important role in the 1969 Apollo 11 space shot that led to the first men landing on the moon, and Neil Armstrong's moonwalk. All the satellite radio signals that allowed communication with the space capsule went through an installation on Grand Turk. The person ostensibly in charge was an Air Force Major who oversaw the civilian workers there; however, the real guy in charge was the Pan American Airways supervisor. I later met astronaut Armstrong on a trip that I will talk about later.

Over the years, I became friends with several people who were stationed at Ascension Island, a tiny, isolated volcanic island in the South Atlantic Ocean. Now part of the British Overseas Territory of St. Helena, Ascension and Tristan da Cunha, it was the site of an important NASA satellite tracking station during the years I was in the Turks and Caicos. Ascension Islanders would sometimes come to visit us and tour our communication facilities. In fact, I knew Major M.E. "John" Wainwright, who was the very first Administrator of Ascension Island from 1964 to 1966. He moved to Grand Turk in 1971, when his brother Robin was Administrator.

In a way, we were sorry to see the old airstrip close in Grand Turk in 1971 because the challenge and entertainment—and danger—of landing disappeared. However, the closing was a good thing for safety's sake. The 5,000-foot-long, asphalt strip was supposed to open at one minute after midnight, exactly 60 seconds after the old one officially closed. So, the idea occurred to us one night that it would be a great feat to make the last takeoff from the Church Folly Street strip and, one minute later, to make the first civilian landing on the Air Force base. And that is exactly what a bunch of us did in the middle of the night.

Making this difficult was the fact that there were no lights for an after-sundown takeoff or landing, which the authorities frowned upon; but, a good time was had by all anyway. In fact, John Houseman, M.B.E., a former Major in the British Army and the editor of *The Conch News*, the Islands' only newspaper, was one of the passengers on board; he insisted on detailing the entire story for all readers of his local newspaper, far and wide.

The tower controller at the base was a civilian who was an Air Force veteran of the Vietnam War, and I became friendly with him. It was this gentleman who first educated me about the concept of the Internet, which was originally a project of the Department of Defense—something called the ARPANET (Advanced Research Projects Agency Network), which went live in 1969.

In fact, that same vet was much impressed by my ability to land a DC-3 in tight or difficult conditions. "Embry, we could have used you in Vietnam," he said, "You fly that thing like a fighter pilot." He went on to suggest that I get in touch with someone for a job with Air America or Civil Air Transport—both were US Central Intelligence Agency (CIA) fronts that supported covert military operations in Southeast Asia. For a very brief minute, I thought about the great pay and excitement that such a job would provide; that is, until I remembered my wife and newborn child. Leaving them and going halfway across the world to a dangerous line of work was not an option.

Interestingly, that was not the only suggestion that I could use my flying ability in a war zone. An English guy I met in the Islands mentioned that he had connections with the Rhodesian Air Force, if I ever wanted to consider flying there. This was during the Rhodesian Bush War, a civil war of sorts that lasted from 1964 to 1979 and pitted three forces against each other. My assignment would be to fly a gunship version of a DC-3. An interesting offer; but once again, no thanks.

In any event, sometime after that runway opening in 1971, Caicos Airways shut down, and I flew for a time for a Dominican outfit owned by James Russell "Jim" Hodge, who originally hailed from upstate New York. His brother Russ was a 1964 Olympian and one-time world record holder in the decathlon; Russ later became a long time assistant coach for the UCLA track team. Their mother Alice Arden Hodge competed in the high jump in the 1936 Olympics in Berlin. Quite an active, athletic group.

Popularly known as "Jimmy the Gringo from Santo Domingo," Jim Hodge was quite a character. Fluent in Spanish, he lived in Santo Domingo and was allegedly in the timber and various other businesses, under the corporate name LASKA. Jim was always vague about what he did, and he would involve himself in any new ventures that came to mind. For that and various other reasons, I often wondered if he was connected to the CIA in some way.

Although Jim wasn't a pilot, he had a small plane which was always flown by a local man. He and his family were very active free- and scuba divers. In fact, I first met him several years earlier when I skin-dived with him in South Caicos. He was involved in importing produce to the Islands. In fact, his family still owns 5 acres on Parrot Cay, which is the center of much new, expensive development.

Once, he, Fritz Ludington and I established and operated a construction company called TICON. We bought a piece of property on Grand Turk, and we constructed a warehouse building to store our cement, steel rods and other necessary materials and equipment—in only 10 days! The locals were quite amazed at the speed and quality of our building. Most of our success in this regard was due to the LCT that Jim employed to transport all our heavy materials. Landing craft, tanks were amphibious vessels used during World War II for carrying and landing tanks on beaches under assault. Perfect for carrying the construction equipment we needed.

We later hired Conor Smythe, Noreen's brother, to supervise our company's daily construction efforts. Conor was a civil engineer, just out of school, so we thought he'd be perfect at that job. He wasn't, but he learned a lot. Conor is now a retired civil engineer who lived in

Edmonton, Alberta with his Canadian wife and two sons until her death around 2012. He's a pretty good guy, and I am still occasionally in touch with him.

The construction company turned out to be a good business; it developed into the largest one in the Turks and Caicos Islands. We were retained to build the local bank, two schools and similar buildings. The company lasted for quite a few years into the 1980s, but it's no longer in business.

Later, around June 1971, Jim decided that he was going to organize and operate a grocery store in Grand Turk and beat everyone else's prices on imported produce. We could deliver various foods from the Dominican Republic or Puerto Rico a whole lot cheaper than anyone could fly it down from Florida. So, we leased an old DC-3 and got into the produce business, trundling back and forth on that plane, importing fruits and vegetables to the Turks and Caicos from Puerto Rico and Santo Domingo. It was very successful until he started getting hit with all the shakedowns by minor government officials, a very common cost of doing business in the West Indies.

On one of these flights, I was flying a DC-3 to Puerto Rico, but I had no license from the Federal Aeronautics Agency (FAA) certifying me to be a legitimate freight carrier. I needed a co-pilot, and that person was Lars, a Swedish kid with only a private pilot's license from Sweden, not the United States. Needless to say, after we landed in San Juan, the FAA inspectors showed up and started walking purposefully toward the plane. Thinking quickly, I sent Lars into the plane's head and told him to be absolutely quiet, and he did so. Meanwhile, when the inspectors asked about my co-plot, I advised them that he was stricken with a rather severe case of diarrhea and had fled to the terminal. They accepted that story, and I had another successful, albeit somewhat illegal, flight.

As I indicated earlier, a lot of what we did back then was illegal—too-short runways, no seat belts, overweight cargo planes, improperly licensed pilots and whatever. But we really didn't consider any of it to be serious at the time, because we knew our jobs and did them well.

On one occasion, I was flying a Citabria 7 with Jim. The Citabria 7 is a light single-engine, two-seat, fixed conventional gear airplane which was first produced in the United States in 1964. Designed for flight training, utility and personal use, it is capable of sustaining significant aerobatic stresses. Its name spelled backwards— airbatic— reflects this.

Well, we were flying over cane fields outside Santo Domingo at the time when Jim started pushing me, "Do a loop, do a loop!" Finally, I caved in to his urging and tried one in the small plane. The first loop was not very good—I stalled at the top of the loop; the second one was much better. Obviously, we both survived—unlike the macho Dominican pilot Manolo who worked for him and flew his plane into a 10,000-foot high mountain in the DR while flying out of Santo Domingo. Not that Manolo was doing loops, just ignoring documented dangerous weather.

That was the same day the Jim and I first saw a Boeing 747 wide-body commercial airliner, a photo of which we saw in the airport. It was so much larger than the 707, it was unbelievable. Although involved with much smaller aircraft, we were duly impressed with the behemoths of the industry.

Operating our flying business in the Dominican Republic back in that day was no problem. Jim knew people and always received permission for us to do business there. Sometimes we used Dominican C-46s and sometimes our own DC-3. The Curtiss C-46 Commando was a rugged cargo transport, built during World War II, that was used by the Dominican Air Force. We also conducted flights out of Puerto Rico quite frequently, flying back to Grand Turk with produce and all sorts of foods.

On one occasion, Jim was arrested for smuggling. But this did not involve illegally trafficking in cocaine, marijuana or any other controlled substance. His illegal substance was *bologna*! For some reason at that time, bologna was on the list of foods that we were forbidden to export, and he was arrested for trying to smuggle some out of the Dominican Republic. It quickly became known to Jim and all his friends as the Great Bologna Smuggling Caper.

One of our employees during that time was a weird co-pilot named Gordon, whom we nicknamed "Flash." He sometimes wore a flight captain's uniform, complete with epaulets. But he was a good pilot—a real natural—and we flew together quite often.

Returning from San Juan once, we were really weighed down with a load of groceries. After takeoff, we were all the way to Mayaquez, which was on the other—western—end of Puerto Rico, before we could climb to an altitude of 2,000 feet. Gordon, who was about 5'6" tall, asked me, "What are we going to do if we lose an engine?" I replied, "Well, Gordon, first we'll have to get rid of some weight. Since I'm bigger than you, I'll run back there and start throwing cargo out, you know, one 50-pound sack of flour at a time." He responded, "No, don't you worry about it—if we ever lose an engine, I'll run back there and throw *three* sacks out at a time!" Despite our apprehension, we never lost an engine during our flying, and we flew many shipments of food into the Islands.

As I indicated, Flash was a really funny guy. Once, he showed up at the British Overseas Airways Corporation (BOAC) counter in Miami wearing that uniform that I referred to above, along with a "Caicos Airways" pilot's ID card, and he requested a complimentary ride to London, based on professional courtesy. Lo and behold, he actually convinced them to let him fly there free! I have no idea whatever happened to him after we parted ways.

Because I started flying for Air Caicos in August of 1971, I didn't make a lot of flights for LASKA. One of the reasons that I can recall the history and circumstances of so many of the flights I made is that I kept all my flight log books. For every flight that I took, I made notations in my log about takeoff, landing, destinations and unusual occurrences. They became mini-diaries or journals for me, and I still refer to them when I want to recall details more accurately than my memory allows.

The last I heard about Jim Hodge some years ago, indicated that he was operating a waste disposal business in Seattle, Washington.

There was an unusual flying occurrence in the late '60s that intrigued me. While flying from Provo to South Caicos, someone in distress broke in on our UNICOM radio frequency. UNICOM is a frequency generally used at airports with a low volume of aviation traffic where no control tower is in use. "Can anyone hear me?" he said. "I'm flying a small, single-engine plane and I'm lost and running out of fuel."

Well, I quickly landed and went to the attic of the Admiral's Arms where a large, powerful radio was kept, and I was able to contact him. He was confused and was describing islands that weren't familiar to me at all. In fact, he was slightly gaga, so to speak. Unable to assist him, I finally heard his last transmission: "Well, I guess I'm going in." Then complete silence.

Later, we verified that a plane was indeed missing. But I always wondered about real story behind that incident. Was someone truly in trouble? Or was someone trying to fake their death and disappear forever? There were certainly plenty of islands in the area on which to land in case of an emergency. It was an odd situation, and it gave me a funny sensation. There never was a follow up, so I will never know the whole truth of what happened.

Anyway, as I said earlier, while working for Jim, another airline—Air Caicos—started operating, using DC3s; so, I hired out my services to them. For a time, we began to think that we were a genuine airline because we had: DC-3s; a Convair 440 Metropolitan, which was really hot stuff in those days; the North Star, a big Canadian version of the DC-4 powered by Rolls Royce Merlin engines; and a couple of Aztecs for charters. As it turned out, we had grown too big and actually had too many planes for the small market we were in. The Convair 440 Metropolitan was a reliable commercial passenger airliner that could seat up to 52 passengers. The Douglas DC-4 Canadair North Star was a popular and reliable, but noisy, propeller-driven airliner that could seat as many as 62 passengers in its heyday. Developed in the 1940's, some of these planes continued to fly into the 1970s, but as cargo carriers.

So, things started going downhill, and maintenance was first on that list. That's always the first thing that gets neglected when an airline starts trying to take economy measures—always remember that, even when considering major airline carriers.

There was another air freight operation in the Islands at the same time called Turks Air, to which I had no connection.

Let me tell you about some crashes or near-crashes in which I was involved.

On November 19, 1968, I crashed the Cessna 180 pretty badly near Conch Bar on a trip with John Wanklyn, a Bahamian employee of McAlpine who was working on the runway improvement project, and Jim Routh, a friend from Long Beach, California. The landing gear collapsed, we hit the brush and the nose went straight down—we all ended up hanging from our seats. Jim said, "That's number 7, let's get the hell out of here." We ended up walking about 10 miles before we could find help. This incident occurred just a month after the engine failure of the Twin Bonanza that I mentioned earlier.

One of the mechanical failures in the late 1960s involved my wife Noreen and Tommy Coleman. I was flying a Cessna 185 Skywagon—a six-seat, single engine plane—with Tommy in the front seat and Noreen, who was reading, in the back. Shortly after takeoff, our only engine went out, and Tommy and I furiously looked at the landscape for a safe, smooth area in which to crash land. As it turned out, I was able to swerve, change direction, glide back to the airstrip and land there. Noreen had been so engrossed in her novel that she had no idea we were in trouble! It turns out that a carburetor cable had been incorrectly installed.

When I was flying for Air Caicos, there was one period beginning in October 1971, when I sustained *four* engine failures in only *ten days* in *two* different DC-3s! Every nightmare a pilot could imagine occurred—from parts failures to loose induction pipes. That was pretty scary. Most pilots can go their entire flying career without one actual engine failure, and I suffered four in that short period. Only the words unbelievable and extraordinary do justice to having all those shutdowns so close to each other.

Just weeks after that, on November 13, 1971, I had two engine failures on the same aircraft in *one day*! I had to feather my DC-3's left engine during a morning flight and safely landed it; our aviation mechanic told me that it had a busted oil line. So, I went to lunch while he repaired it; then I returned and took off for my next stop. Not long after I was on my way, my right engine quit. After feathering it and successfully landing, we determined that it was a cylinder failure.

Speaking of crashes, no one really took seriously the idea of planes and ships mysteriously disappearing in the so-called Bermuda Triangle, located somewhat to the north of Haiti and Puerto Rico. We basically believed that plane crashes and losses were due to human error, navigational mistakes or systems and equipment failure.

As far as crash options went, the Turks and Caicos were fairly flat and not mountainous, plus there was a lot of water present. Despite that, the upkeep and dependability of the aircraft parts and equipment started to significantly increase my anxiety. It was about that time that I began to nervously realize that I was mortal, made of flesh and blood, and that I might not escape the next engine mishap with my life.

That brings to mind Edwin Taylor, a local guy whom I met during my flying days in the Islands. His father was a police sergeant whose popular nickname was "Uncle Ben" due to his similarity to the rice-character. Having obtained his commercial pilot's license, Edwin went to work for us flying the local Turks and Caicos routes. Then, in preparation for moving him to one of our international routes, we sent him to advanced flying school in Florida, where he did well and passed all his examinations.

However, in August 1973, disaster befell him. He was flying a Britten-Norman Islander on a trip from Port-au-Prince to Grand Turk when he encountered bad weather and must have forgotten a primary rule of flying: "When in doubt, chicken out." Eyewitnesses said that the plane broke up in midair due to an extremely intense local thunderstorm, and it crashed near Dondon in North Haiti. All 10 people on board were killed, including Taylor and Tony Perella, the mechanic.

Just two days prior to that crash, Noreen and I had flown to Ireland with the kids for a vacation; little Embry was only six months old. Upon hearing the devastating news of the accident, I immediately booked a return Aer Lingus flight from Ireland to New York to Miami to Grand Turk. Then I flew to Haiti where I connected with David Dumont, our acting manager at that time, and we travelled together by car, donkey and foot to the crash site in the mountains. Upon arrival, there really wasn't much to see, because the wreckage had already been stripped of anything salvageable by the locals.

In addition to the devastating loss of ten lives, this was a very horrific incident for us on several levels, both personally and as an air service. Edwin was a good kid and we greatly regretted his loss. We were later required to give testimony to the aviation authorities at a hearing in Cap-Haïtien; also, we were also named as defendants in a civil lawsuit filed by Edwin's family. Eventually, that suit was rightfully dismissed—at every step of the way, the crash was determined by the authorities to be pilot error, as it was in reality.

There is a postscript to Edwin's sad story. By the time Noreen and I returned to the Islands in the late 1990s, Edwin's older brother, Derek Hugh Taylor, had become Chief Minister of the Turks and Caicos, a position he held from 1995 to 2003. Since Noreen and I were going to be residing there for a time, I thought it was incumbent upon me to pay a call to Chief Minister Taylor, and I did so to pay my respects. Upon meeting with him, I informed him that I still thought about the crash and the loss of his brother, and that I was very sorry about it. He listened graciously and advised me, "It was not your fault. We are good."

In spite of those unsettling crashes and anxious reflections, I truly enjoyed my job. There were many good times in Caicos; it wasn't all just crappy airplanes with engines shutting down and crashes. There were a lot of good-hearted people with whom I worked and knew, and we moved an abundance of freight and passengers to their destinations, safe and sound. Plus, we had regularly scheduled runs to Nassau, which was always a fun trip. I never let my safety concerns become unreasonable fears.

Chapter 8: Pine Cay Characters

During all these years and adventures that I have related, Provident, Ltd. was continually operating in Providenciales and achieving success. Fritz Ludington was improving the hotel, finishing the airstrip, completing the roads and, at long last, selling some land parcels so that he could start to earn some return on investment for all the partners who had trusted him with their money. The Islands were starting to develop, and some people started to believe that Fritz wasn't as crazy as he seemed, what with his constructing hotels and considering residential house construction.

"I think it was the beginning of 1960, Provident, Ltd. came in," former Legislative Council member Gustavus Lightbourne stated, but it was actually 1966. "I later learned that Fritz (Ludington) had been eyeing these Islands for eight years, but there was no way of landing. He used to fly over, but there was no way of landing, unless you landed in South Caicos and took a boat over to the Islands. The first person I saw was Tommy Coleman—he came here in a small boat from South Caicos…When he asked for the person who represented the Island, they told him that person was me, and he came to search me out…They wanted 4,000 acres of land, and they would develop it… This was the single most important economic development of Providenciales and therefore the rest of the Islands."

Longtime political leader Hilly Ewing from Blue Hills recalled, "Provident, Ltd. was committed to the government to build some roads, mostly in exchange for land. So, they got to work from Blue Hills to the Provident, Ltd. site and everywhere Provident has property. They built subdivision roads, airport roads and private runways. We built the first airport road by hand—where one-engine planes could land. I was one of the contractors with Ray Ward."

My friend Bill Clare from South Caicos stated, "Third Turtle Inn was doing very good…people started coming in to do diving and also to do bone fishing…A lot of persons bought property here and they started building private homes—Ray Ward and Doc Withey started building homes for persons."

As all this work was going on, my path was crossing with many unique and colorful individuals, including those mentioned above. The following is a brief look at some of them.

§

By 1970, we were actually able to land on real airstrips; that is, 3,000-foot gravel runways on Middle Caicos and North Caicos and at Providenciales. There was also an airport at Pine Cay, a small island located between North Caicos and Provo. That area was being developed by: The Countess Helen Czernin, an Ohio native who became Austrian aristocracy by virtue of her marriage to Count Ferdinand Czernin; architect George Nipanich from Poland, a friend of the Count's; and several other off-the-wall strange people. In 1960, Hurricane Donna, which hit the Turks and Caicos Islands hard, cut a channel between Pine Cay and Little Water Cay.

The Count died in 1966 of a heart attack, before I ever had the pleasure of meeting him. After that, my friend Tommy Coleman and Countess Helen became a couple for years; they lived on Parrot Cay, located north of Pine Cay, just off North Caicos. Their relationship ended when she decided to live on Grand Turk.

Pine Cay was a beautiful island setting. In addition to being peaceful and quiet, it was old money, as opposed to Parrot Cay, which was flashy and yelled new money. About 500 acres in size, Pine Cay contained a fresh water pond—the only one in the Islands—and extremely beautiful beaches. Its owners were developing it into a private, exclusive resort, with a small but tasteful clubhouse and various residential housing sites of 5 to 10 acres each.

Tommy Coleman recalled, "I was the King of Parrot Cay for 14 years. We made up our own rules and no one bothered us. The Governor used to come over on holidays with the kids and visit us. The whole time I was there, there was no one else there."

On one memorable journey to Pine Cay, George Nipanich and I set sail from South Caicos across the banks—meaning a straight-line voyage from east to west— on an old, locally-built sloop, an overnight trip of about 44 nautical miles or 50 miles standard. The hired hands running the boat were all from North Caicos; they had a compass, but kept it carefully wrapped up in a rag down in the hold. They generally navigated by the stars and only produced the compass if they were really lost.

Anyway, George and I sat up most of the night talking; he told me tales about growing up in his Polish homeland, and how he had served in the Polish underground during World War II. Skilled at masquerading in various uniforms and clothes, he once journeyed to Paris through the Nazi lines while disguised as a Nazi SS Captain; another time, he travelled as a Colonel in the French Army. George was truly an articulate, fascinating guy.

After arriving at Pine Cay, in anticipation of spending several days there, George gave me the grand tour of the Island. One lazy evening we were sitting around, listening to stories told by the local fellows from North Caicos who were employed there. During one discussion, they started talking about eyesight, and the topic of glass eyes arose. One fellow resolutely stated, "Well, they're no damn good at all! My uncle lost his eye, and bought a glass eye, and he couldn't see at all out of the damned thing—he really got gypped!" I thought that George and I were going to fall down laughing—the fellow was quite serious.

George was also quite a ladies' man. Once he showed up at the South Caicos airfield to meet a knockout gorgeous woman named Maru, a Pan Am hostess whom he eventually married. She was of Eastern European or Russian origin, and everyone who saw her commented about how good-looking she was.

Around 1979, after I had returned to the States, I had occasion to meet and reminisce with George after he and Maru moved to Coral Gables, Florida.

§

Now, back to the Islands. Eventually, an Englishman named Charles William "Liam" Maguire became very involved in the development of Pine Cay. A very high-energy, humorous gentleman, Liam originally came to the Turks and Caicos as a surveyor or civil engineer on some special project with the British Royal Engineers and decided to remain. This was long before the big influx of Royal Engineers who arrived in 1969-70 with their heavy equipment to resurface the airstrip. Liam opened a small hotel called the Admiral's Arms in South Caicos and had been making a go of it in business there for years. He also had become a Legislative Council member by 1974, and later served as the Minister of Tourism and Development.

A very popular place to hang out, the Admiral's Arms comprised 10 or 12 hotel rooms plus a bar and was located in an old salt proprietor's house from the early 1800s that overlooked the harbor.

Liam called his development business the Caicos Company Ltd, and he was the managing director. His partners included David Lindsay, Jr., publisher of the Sarasota, Florida *Herald-Tribune*, who had also started an aviation business that refurbished ex-military P-51s into well-equipped civilian business aircraft; my friend Norman Saunders from South Caicos, a long-time politician who would later become Chief Minister of the Turks and

Caicos; and, Alden Charles Durham from South Caicos, a politician, future councilman and government official.

Eventually, Liam expanded his operations by opening a small store selling groceries and sundries and several other operations, including a bank. However, the refueling operation at the airport continued to be his main money-maker. At that time, South Caicos was a major refueling point between South and North America for all types of executive aircraft, crop dusters, and other planes. Oftentimes, their pilots would stay over at the Arms for the night after enjoying a drink or two in an Island watering hole. Of course, Liam was always ready to pump that 100-octane Esso fuel at any time of day to any aircraft that might land there.

"Liam got into the refueling business, grocery store, hotel, hardware store, bank and electricity," my friend Lynette Mills Bassett recalled, "That was the turning point for the Turks and Caicos. He used a lot of local people, and he used some expatriate."

Islander "Speed" Gardiner agreed with that assessment. "Maguire helped with the survey of the Island. He was a force to be reckoned with. He made a lot of difference in the Turks and Caicos Islands, especially in South Caicos and Pine Cay. He was a very outstanding person in the community. Everyone who wanted work went to look for Maguire, and he would find work for them. If we had more people like Maguire, we would be further ahead."

Bill Clare's simple summary was accurate: "You have to understand that without Liam and Fritz (Ludington), we would not have been here today."

There's a side story about Liam's bank. One should remember that there weren't an abundance of rules and regulations in the Islands at that time. Although Liam had convinced one of his American investors in the fuel business to put up the capital, he himself didn't know that much about banking. To address that lack of knowledge, he brought in Doug Doherty, a trained banker from

Pennsylvania, to assist him. In spite of Doug's abilities, it was still a questionable operation. On one occasion, one of the Islanders mentioned to me that he had taken his paycheck to the bank to cash it, but was denied a withdrawal. Why? Liam's faithful Englishwoman-teller matter-of-factly told the customer, "No withdrawals today—only deposits."

Today, the Islands have the reputation of offering a variety of attractive financial services. That's mostly because in 1970, the United Kingdom declared the Turks & Caicos Islands an official offshore center. This designation means that there are no taxes on income or capital gains, no inheritance or estate taxes, and strict confidentiality laws regarding bank accounts. Or, as Tommy Coleman later put it, "You are probably looking at the newest, richest little city in this world…when you consider the tax haven and the billions of dollars that are shipped through here."

Liam was a real pistol, all very stiff-upper-lip-British, with a fervent show-the-Union Jack-attitude. Noreen and I dined at the Admiral's Arms maybe once a week, and it always turned into an assembly of the masses. Everyone—hotel guests, locals dining out and whomever else showed up—would file through the buffet-style line in the main dining room, obtain their food and drink, then sit together family-style at a huge, 25-foot long table, over which Liam would preside. When he rang a little bell, the servers would pop out of the kitchen with wines and various other culinary delights. Overseeing this dining congregation, on the wall right behind Liam, was a large painting, or reproduction, of Lord Horatio Nelson, hero of the British Navy, who had led an expeditionary party to the Caicos Islands early in his career (1777), and fought the French after they had captured Grand Turk's salt works (1783). The whole dinner scene was just the damnedest thing—like it belonged in the previous century with all its action and energy.

When I was in England several years ago, I visited Portsmouth to see HMS *Victory*, Lord Nelson's flagship during his epic victory over the French and Spanish in the Battle of Trafalgar. What a ship-of-the-line that was!

Never wanting the area to become too Americanized, Liam and his ventures accomplished many good things for the Islands; however, he never made a hefty profit; in fact, he may have lost money. That may be the reason that he eventually emigrated to the States. Although he had developed considerable plans for South Caicos, it appears that he just arrived a few years too early. Liam eventually passed away due to some type of eye cancer; he was never known to wear sunglasses in all the sunshiny places in which he lived.

§

Charles Shepard "Doc" Withey II was originally from Grand Rapids, Michigan. In 1969, he and his wife Margaret ("Peggy") were en route to Puerto Rico in their private plane when they stopped to refuel and spend the night in Provo. They liked it so much that they decided to stay. They became friends of mine. He was a smart guy and a hard worker.

Doc flew a Republic RC-3 Seabee, an all-metal one-engine amphibious sports aircraft with four seats. It was unique for its boxlike forward cabin, a high wing with a two-bladed propeller in pusher configuration and a long, slender tail boom. Built prior to 1948, these aircraft became popular bush planes. I never flew a Republic Seabee, but I did earn my float plane rating around that time. It was in a Piper Cub on floats in Biscayne Bay off Miami, Florida. That aircraft was certainly not over-powered!

At first, Doc and his wife decided to build a vacation home on Provo. However, the following year, they permanently moved their entire family to the Islands. He began working as a commercial contractor, which is what he did in the States. Trained as an electrical engineer, he established Provo Power Company, the first power generating enterprise in the Islands. The need for a permanent medical facility on the Island led Peggy to aid in establishing the Providenciales Health Medical Center, the first such facility to bring North American medicine to the Islands. Jill Söderqvist's mother Bonnie, a medical doctor, and her husband were the prime movers in that project. Jill was married to my friend Bengt Söderqvist.

In any event, Doc and Peggy were compassionate and exemplary people. Doc passed away in 2002 in Palm Beach Gardens, Florida, and Peggy died in 2016 in Indiantown, Florida.

§

There were a lot of memorable stories that originated in the Admiral's Arms dining room, but one in particular involved fellow Englishman John Houseman, the editor whom I mentioned earlier. Houseman, no relation to the famous actor of the same name, had quite an impressive background. Graduating from Oxford with a degree in paleontology, he then attended Sandhurst, the Royal Military Academy, where he won the Sword of Honor, awarded to the best officer cadet in the course. Assigned to Greece during World War II, he was at one time the youngest major in the British Army.

Coming to the Islands around 1969, John became the editor of *The Conch News*. His early newspaper editions consisted of 6-8 mimeographed sheets; he attempted to make a profit by selling advertising space.

Anyway, old John had kind of gone to hell, boozing a little too much after coming to live in the colonies, don't you know. He and his wife Mary Ann could be found with their two children, all four of them usually naked, at their home-front in East Caicos, near the ruins of the settlement of Jacksonville, once home to cattle, sisal and guano industries. They lived on an old, huge sisal plantation; sisal is a plant, its fiber is used in making rope, twine and other products.

His wife and children only lasted there for about a year, probably due to their isolated location on East Caicos, which is basically an 18-square mile, uninhabited island. That brings to mind one of his most memorable quotes, which was directed at me for one of my periodic flying habits.

Knowing what a great figure Mary Ann had, when I flew mail into them with my Cessna 180 letter-carrier—occasionally placing a banana or some fruit in the package for the kids—I would make sure to come in low from the west, with the bright evening sun directly behind me. After taking a sufficiently long look, I would rev the engine loudly to let them know that I was there. Talking to me later about my postal routine, John would just shake his head, saying, "From out of the sun, comes the wily Hun."

Another humorous Houseman quote comes to mind. With a large group in attendance around the dining table at the Arms one evening, Liam was acting a bit pompous about something or another. After tasting the wine, he passed a glass to Houseman to try. The latter took a mouthful, swirled it around in his mouth, ran it in and out of his teeth and then sniffed away at it. After completing this whole stage-worthy performance, Houseman finally spat the wine on the floor, shouting "Bilge, Maguire, bloody bilge!" Of course, the whole place just absolutely cracked up laughing out loud. Perhaps some of our visitors from the States were clueless about what was happening, but the regulars greatly enjoyed the performances. That was not an unusual evening at the Admiral's Arms.

§

Back to Doug Doherty—the banker from Pennsylvania—for a moment. When his job assisting Liam at the latter's bank ended, Doug wanted to remain in the Islands; so, when I was starting up the airline in Haiti (more about this later), I ended up hiring him to supervise and manage Turks and Caicos Airways on Grand Turk. As an aside, this was back when streaking was a popular fad or phenomenon, beginning in 1973 or so. Suffice it to say that our staid American banker-type ended up running naked down the middle of Front Street one memorable night.

Later, he met a teacher from the Dominican Republic who was visiting Noreen and me one winter, and he fell in love with her. His future wife—Franny—had also dated Jim Hodge, so we knew her from the DR. Upon returning to the States with her, Doug ended up doing very well; he owns and operates four McDonald's franchises in Williamsport, Pennsylvania.

§

Two English friends whom we knew in the Islands were Sheila and Robert "Robin" Laing, who moved there in the late '60s or early '70s. Robin came from the family that owned—and later sold—McVitie & Price, the famous British biscuit-maker established in Scotland in 1830. It's now called McVitie's and is a British snack food brand owned by United Biscuits. He had previously worked in boat-building and general marine engineering on the Isle of Wight.

Although Sheila worked for us for a brief time as an agent for Caicos Airways on Grand Turk, the Laings were fairly well off and enjoyed the sailing and leisure lifestyle of the area, having first lived in the Bahamas. Sheila also served as the station manager on Grand Turk for Mackey International Airline, which provided direct DC-6 service between the Islands and Miami. Mackey was a big deal—it offered the first service directly from Miami to the Islands, and it used large DC-6 airliners. We were not in competition with them, so Sheila could work for both of us.

"You had to clear the strips of donkeys," Shelia later recalled, "The local boys would come and help me. There was always a cross wind, so carrying a sheet of plywood across the strip could be very difficult. We didn't have any scale, so one learned by going up to TIMCO (Turks Island Import Company) that a case of soda weighed 23 pounds, and that's how I learned weight. I used to do ticketing from the house...Sometime people would come to buy tickets and your hands would be covered in dough (from

119

making bread). In 1972, Mackey International started flying from America—before that, everyone had to come via the Bahamas. But in 1972, we started direct flights from the States—by then the Pan Am strip became accessible to the rest of us, and that's what started it. Easy access to the Island." The Pan Am strip that Sheila refers to is the one at the U.S. Air Force base that I discussed in the previous chapter.

Earlier, Jim Hodge's friend Bill Bivin and I helped the Laings bring down their 45-foot Egg Harbor Sport Fisherman vessel—*The Far Cry*—from the Bahamas. The four of us had a nice ride on those big twin diesel engines. The Laings were captivated by the laid-back charm of Grand Turk.

The Laings started a company called General Trading Company that did business with Provident, Ltd. "We were pleased with Provident," Sheila recalled years later, "We were agents for all kinds of things in 'General Trading'… custom brokerage, insurance, you name it…We imported things that anybody wanted—that's why it was called General Trading."

§

Bill Bivin led an interesting life. A former smoke-jumping firefighter in Montana, he was introduced to the West Indies when he served with the Peace Corps in the Dominican Republic. Falling in love with a local woman on Grand Turk, he stayed in the Islands, supervising the daily activities of the TICON Construction Company prior to Conor Smythe holding that job. Bill later moved to Alaska, became Chairman of the Board of the State Chamber of Commerce and was tragically killed in a plane crash in 1993. Ironically, one of his favorite humorous sayings was "Those cumulo-granite clouds will get you!" In his honor, the Bill Bivin Award is presented to an individual who exemplifies a citizen through volunteer work that is most significant to the community of Bethel, Alaska.

§

Now, back to my experiences at Pine Cay. Geologically, there weren't rocks of any type on that island, which was just a large sand bar; so, the runway there was actually just sand. As more planes landed on it over time, the sand fell apart and became spongy. We had to keep moving the runway, maneuvering from side to side, until finally the whole situation became absolutely unbearable and hopeless. I don't know what ever happened with the damn thing—if they worked out any of its issues by adding stones or rocks—but years ago, I swore that I wouldn't dare to land an airplane there even on a bet!

Having said that, I do believe that Bob Galvin took a Piper Cub out of there one morning, but, as Noreen's Irish family may have said, "He had drink taken." He was another one of those interesting guys with whom I crossed paths in the Islands. Bob, who flew for us at Caicos Airways for a while, was very intelligent and came from a good—and wealthy—family. Unfortunately, his own father didn't think Bob was worth a damn, and daddy established a trust fund with a couple of million dollars in it for his son, with the condition that Bob couldn't access it until he was 40 years old. Because Bob knew he had the future made, he simply enjoyed flying and living for the moment. Although he was a good pilot—even in DC-3s—he did tend to imbibe too much on a regular basis.

Prior to working for us for us, Bob had flown a DC-3 into Grand Turk for some other outfit, but the ground crew there didn't want to allow him to take off because he was clearly impaired. Whereupon Sheila and Robin Laing rounded me up somewhere and enlisted my help.

In an interesting turn of events, I decided that the only way to stop him from flying was to get him even drunker. At my direction, the Laings maneuvered him to the local Turks Head Inn and proceeded to get him even more intoxicated. Then Sheila pleaded, "We gotta get this airplane out of here, Embry. Do you mind stealing it from Galvin and taking it back to its home base in Provo?"

That presented no problem for me, so I got in the cockpit, warmed up the engines, secured the plane and locked the cockpit cabin door. Then the Laings and my friend Bob Kellogg trundled poor, besotted Bob out of the Turks Head Inn and deposited him on the plane. Kellogg was there to hammer Galvin around a little bit and persuade him to sit down. Kellogg directed him, "Sit down or I'll put you down!" So, Galvin became just a passenger as I took off and proceeded to deliver his plane back to the owners. Kellogg also flew along, for good measure; it was never difficult to hitch a ride home with someone.

By the way, the Turks Head Inn was built around 1830 as a private home and was later used as the guest house for the British governor, and then as the American consulate. Today, it's a privately-owned boutique hotel, with a pretentious "e" on the end of it—Inne—and I wouldn't give too much credence to the Inn's history as briefly related on their website. I do know that it was the only hotel in the Turks and Caicos prior to the Admiral's Arms; and, it was a popular gathering place for various ex-pats.

§

Fritz Ludington had originally met Bob Kellogg in Georgetown, Great Exuma in the Bahamas. Kellogg was another in the long line of wonderful characters whom I met during my years in the West Indies. He had travelled to that region, maybe from Michigan, for a sailing vacation, liked the island way of life and resided there for many years.

Kellogg eventually took his sailboat back to Florida, sold it and bought another unique vessel. Named the *Anna*, it was an old Swedish coastal schooner, a wooden motor vessel about 90- or 120-feet long. It was powered by a huge diesel engine, which had to be started with an explosive charge, such as a shotgun shell. It was necessary for Kellogg to screw the shell into the cylinder and whack it with a hammer; with that, it would explode and start the engine rolling. That may sound a bit odd, but it really did work. Actually, I looked it up once and found that this method has an official name: The Coffman engine starter, AKA shotgun starter.

Bob Kellogg was proud to be the Captain of the *Anna*, but that command didn't last long. He was in the process of transporting freight, including building materials, from Florida to Providenciales when he went aground just off Provo; maybe it was just the first or second run that he made. Everybody pitched in but still had one hell of a time unloading all the cargo, and the *Anna* just never got going again. The whole unfortunate incident became kind of a running joke. Despite that setback, Kellogg still stayed around.

Everyone gave Kellogg the nickname "Captain Crunch" for rather obvious reasons—he was a boat captain and his name was Kellogg, same as the cereal maker. He was always Captain Crunch to all who knew him. While working as a stevedore up in the Great Lakes area, Kellogg had developed a cocky attitude that he was tough as nails, and then some. He performed odd jobs, helped run the airline for a time and served as sort of a general assistant to Fritz; in the corporate world, he would have been called an executive assistant or something similar. Sometimes, he even captained the *Seven Dwarfs*.

Once, Jim Hodge, his girlfriend-of-the-month Myrna, Noreen and I hatched an idea to set out on a fishing expedition. Filled with the spirit of adventure, I said, "Let's see if Kellogg can take us out on the *Seven Dwarfs*." Sure enough, Bob thought this was a gas of an idea, and so we all departed for the high seas. Jim, Myrna, Noreen and I arrived at the designated time with various groceries, beverages, sleeping items and other expedition necessities. Meanwhile, Kellogg showed up with a carton of Pall Mall cigarettes and two bottles of gin. He merely figured that there was plenty of food available in the ocean, no need to worry about this provision nonsense. So, the five of us departed for French Cay, which was just a tiny sandbar with a reef surrounding it. We did some diving, caught a lot of fish, drank some gin and had a great time for three days.

After Fritz died (more on that shortly), Kellogg relocated to Haiti and ended up raising tobacco on a huge plantation near Cap-Haïtien. He was there for quite a few years before getting into some kind of hassle with the local government officials. Whether he got kicked out of Haiti or just got pissed off and left, I'm not sure. But he eventually wound up near Sarasota, Florida, working with an import company.

For many years after leaving the Islands and returning to the States to run Champion, I maintained contact with Bob and his family. In the early 1980s, Bob was passing through Louisville, driving the import company's delivery van from Florida to Michigan, and he spent a few days reminiscing with me. It was nice to see him, but it just wasn't the same—it was as if the exciting, interesting times in his life were over and done with. He wasn't doing work that he enjoyed, nor was he happy. Unable to recapture that invigorating feeling that he had in the Islands, he was restless and discontented. A kind of gap had developed between us, because I too had experienced all those great times in the Islands, but I had moved on and was pleased— and excited—about being involved in other pursuits. Then, as now, I was enjoying life and still having a good time on my own terms, in my own way. The reason for my pleasure could have been my children, or the farm, or the company or whatever. The truth is that so much of my happiness came from being married to Noreen, who was a great partner.

In 1985, Bob and his mother visited my wife Noreen and me in Louisville when they were on their way to a family wedding in Toledo, Ohio. Shortly after that visit, I received a phone call from his mother informing me that she had found my number in his address book, and she thought I would want to know that Bob had died. That was a terrible shock to me. My friend was only 50 years old but had suffered a sudden and fatal heart attack.

§

During those Island years, there were a multitude of exceptional, unconventional or just plain weird friends and characters appearing in my life. Noreen and I had a friend named David Scott, who had travelled with Sir Robert McAlpine Construction Company—the worldwide English-based company founded in 1869—and was the engineer in charge of paving the runway at the South Caicos airstrip circa 1969. The decision had been made to resurface the original gravel runway with asphalt. It is sufficient to say that this event caused great excitement among not just the airmen like me, but all the locals.

Our friend's entire name was David Hamilton Scott, AOFB. We asked about the title that followed his name. David explained that his father once reviewed a resume that David, early in his professional career, had sent during a job search. His father added AOFB after his son's name, to distinguish it from a crowded field of applicants. Between the two of them, it stood for Ancient Order of Froth Blowers. And, yes, it secured him the job at McAlpine that led him to the islands. Which reminds me, the Islanders all pronounced the company name as "Mac-el-PINE."

Speaking of McAlpine, when in England in 1994, by pure coincidence, I ended up hunting on the grounds of the first Sir Robert McAlpine, 1st Baronet, who was nicknamed "Concrete Bob." That name resulted from him being a pioneer in the use of concrete and labor-saving machinery. His construction business is still in operation today.

Having been invited up to Government House for drinks one afternoon, David was questioned closely by Commissioner Ben Bolt: "Just what are you going to pave the runway with?" Scott hoisted up his Heineken bottle and replied, "Heineken bottles, and I'm doing my best here to see that we have enough—where's the next one?" Although he did not make an overwhelming impression on the District Commissioner with that remark, David was nevertheless a roaring, first-rate guy.

After Noreen and I married, David met my new wife and thought she was wonderful. Likewise, Noreen was kind to him, always helping him bake cakes and all sorts of other tasty goodies. Later, David fell in love with a young lady named Tina Fulford who lived on South Caicos. That enchanting young lady fueled a mad competition between David and Berkeley Barron, who flew for a competing cargo line. Barron had flown Lancaster Bombers for the Royal Air Force during the War and had fought in the Battle of Britain; and he too was madly in love with the alluring Miss Tina. David returned to England. Berkeley won.

§

Although David left the West Indies after the runway project was completed, McAlpine stayed around, winning bids to build roads and some other infrastructure items in the Islands. John Wanklyn, the Bahamian employee of McAlpine who was in the crash that I mentioned earlier, moved to South Caicos and took over these projects. Noreen and I quickly became friends with him and Pat, his English wife. Both were respectable, kind people. Not long ago, I connected with John and had lunch with him; he now lives in Delray Beach, Florida and celebrated his 50th year with McAlpine.

§

The District Commissioner, Ben Bolt, had formerly served as a Group Captain with the Royal Air Force during World War II; he was a really fine fellow whose wife and daughter Pippin lived with him. His daughter, about 20 years old, didn't stay long in the islands—I don't think it was to her taste or liking.

A brief word about government administrators: There was the Governor, the colonial civil servant who oversaw both the Bahamas and the Turks and Caicos; then came the Administrator, who oversaw all the Turks and Caicos Islands; then District Commissioner Bolt, who governed just the Caicos Islands, which had maybe 1,800 citizens at the time.

Commissioner Bolt lived at Government House, situated on a slight, rolling hill. One evening, Noreen and I were invited to their very well-appointed residence for dinner. We happened to be babysitting 2-year-old Paul Dempsey for Noreen's sister at the time, so we took him along. Arriving at the house, we made Paul comfortable in one of the Bolt's spare bedrooms, and he quickly went to sleep. When the evening ended, Noreen and I started out the door, when Mrs. Bolt gently asked, "Excuse me, Noreen, perhaps you forgot something?" We did—Paul. Oops.

§

Sad to say, Fritz Ludington died one month short of his 45th birthday, not long after my family and I left the Islands to return to the States. His gravestone in Birmingham, Alabama reads "ashes scattered at sea." I'm told that they were scattered around Delray Beach, Providenciales and other Turks and Caicos areas. Years later, when I had returned and was living in the Islands with Noreen, I walked into a room and, lo and behold, there was Fritz! Only it was not Fritz, but his son "Boots," red-faced and a little overweight—a dead ringer for his father.

Hilly Ewing, noted Turks and Caicos leader from Blue Hills, observed that the main event that brought about economic progress in the Islands, was "...in the '50s and '60s when Fritz Ludington came to Provo...let's give the devil what's due to him...The company (Provident) came in and did the development, and here is the result from it...Fritz didn't live to see all of the beauty of it, but the good and the bad would go together, as there were some things that happened good and some bad."

§

One character in a class by himself whom I saw a lot in both Delray Beach and the Islands was "Almost Honest" Ed Hegner, an auto parts dealer and hardware store owner from Florida. Ed's other nickname was "Sweet Lips," due to his ability to sell anything to anyone. For example, as Gustav Lightbourne recalled, "Fruits were coming in from the DR—this was difficult to manage as I didn't have proper storage. Ed Hegner started bringing in frozen stuff, and he supplied us with an ice chest to keep the meat."

For a while, Hegner operated Provo Air Service; he did a lot of flying in a Twin Beech D-18, in which he transported auto parts and other supplies, but never any cargo or materials for us. Ed kept his sole plane at Palm Beach County Airpark, commonly called Lantana Airport, overseen by Florida AirMotive.

Once, several of us watched Ed take off in a plane so overloaded with supplies that he actually did not leave the ground until he was in the grass strip at the end of the runway; then, he just barely cleared the four-foot fence that surrounded the field. Up, up, ever so slowly he went—but I guess he eventually made it because I never heard a crash. Those of us present just turned our backs, unable to watch the end. Someone once told me that his business card read: "Ed Hegner: Cargo-Air Charters-Thrill Rides." How apt and true a description.

§

Another unique personality I briefly dealt with was John Hervey, 7th Marquess of Bristol, a British hereditary peer, aristocrat and businessman. A charming fellow, he had come to the Islands with a development plan for hotels and other commercial enterprises, and I flew him around for a while. When he returned a few months later, I was surprised that he recognized and greeted me so readily when he disembarked from his Bahamas Airways plane.

Shortly after that, Robin Wainwright, the Islands' Administrator, cautioned me by saying, "Be careful, the Marquess is not all he seems to be." Robin was correct. The Marquess had a terrible upbringing, was badly mistreated by his father and became horribly addicted to cocaine and other drugs. He had served time in jail and had declared bankruptcy. My suspicion now is that he was scouting the Islands for possible opportunities to further his drug dealing. It is amazing what people can turn into.

§

I used to know a local guy from Provo named Dan Capron, who was working in the fishing and construction business. However, I remember him mostly from his playing the bass washtub and the saw in local bands.

Providenciales was an attractive, but boring place before the roads were built, and my friend Bengt Söderqvist and I were always looking for entertainment. We'd hear about a gig someone was playing, jump on my motorcycle and off we went to some tiny village where a band was playing. Dan Capron was often in those bands.

§

That brings to mind another Capron—Cyril "Hearts" Capron-who ran a small bar in the village of Blue Hills on Provo. You could go there for rum and tobacco smuggled in from Haiti. The tobacco was unique—it came in a large, solid block from which you'd have to scrape off small pieces with your knife, then hand-roll them into a cigarette. Hearts also had a kerosene refrigerator which, thankfully, meant cold beer and soft drinks—a real delicacy in the Islands.

§

I've mentioned before about how some visitors to the Islands fell prey to drinking as a solution to the boredom—or other problems—that they faced in the Islands. My friend Tommy Coleman mentioned that issue in my 2005 interview with him. Tommy concluded," I am glad that I didn't turn out to be the drunk that I thought I was going to be."

By the way, Tommy died in 2013. I had many good times with him. I'm glad I went to Florida and spent some time with him a few weeks before he died.

§

In the Preface to this story, I briefly referred to the tract of land that we had partial ownership rights to in the Islands, near Conch Bar in Middle Caicos. How we acquired this parcel is quite a story.

It seems that a friend of mine, a local fellow named Onward Christian Soldiers Hamilton— "Onward" for short—approached me once with a deal. Now, Onward was a sailing boat captain with a reputation as a wheeler-dealer, so I was somewhat skeptical from the beginning. He explained that he needed to buy a truck to use on South Caicos, and he wanted to borrow the needed funds from me. Although Onward was shady to a certain degree, his sister, whom I liked and appreciated, was quite a success story. From a little village of 50 people—Conch Bar—she had studied in Belgium, become a doctor and married there. It was neat to find someone who did so well from humble origins on Turks and Caicos.

After deciding to assist him, I asked for some type of collateral. Whereupon Onward agreed to give me the rights to 10 of the 40 acres that he owned in Middle Caicos, on a ridge overlooking the Island, with a view of the sea.

Sad to say, Onward never repaid me, and the truck eventually quit running; even sadder, he then died, leaving a legal mess and many children to fight with me over control of the property. I ended up donating my legal right to the 10 acres to the local Turks and Caicos Museum for their use, believing that would help straighten out the legal jumble. In any event, upon returning years later with Noreen to evaluate the property, I figured out, sure enough, that it would have been unfeasible to build there—no roads, no stores and a whole bunch of mosquitoes. An unrealistic piece of paradise, but with a view.

§

Earlier, I mentioned another pilot whom I got to know quite well—Harold Bruce "Berkeley" Barron, the former Royal Air Force flier who later became a flight instructor for the United States Air Force. Berkeley was married twice and both of his wives were named Tina—one from Argentina, and the second, to whom he was married for the rest of his life, from Turks and Caicos.

Berkeley was a first-class fellow. He flew for Turks and Caicos Airlines for a good while, and was one of the pilots who went to Haiti to work with us, as I'll discuss later. Flying one of those loud DC-4 North Stars with the four earsplitting Rolls-Royce Merlin engines—basically four of the engines that the World War II British Spitfire fighter plane used—he would scream right by the exterior of the Admiral's Arms bar, maybe only 20 feet over the water!

For a time, he worked for David Lindsey in Sarasota, converting single-seat P-51 Mustangs to double seats. Eventually he retired, but remained in South Caicos. After his death, I donated a plaque to the local Anglican church in his memory. It began, "Captain H.B. Berkeley Barron, early aviator in these Islands..."

§

Closely observing all these shenanigans from 1968 to 1975 was Mr. V. H. "Andy" Anderson, Chief of the Royal Turks and Caicos Islands Police Force. He was a first-rate law enforcement chap whom I appreciated a lot. Andy came to the Islands after being recruited by the United Kingdom's Home Office—responsible for safety and security of its subjects—from a stint with the British Colonial Service in Africa. Interestingly, this Island peacekeeping agency was established in 1799, making it one of the oldest police forces in the world.

§

A final, final note about Lew Whinnery: After I stopped flying out of Puerto Rico, I lost track of Lew; however, when I was in Miami later, I heard a rumor that he was also there. Sure, enough, when I checked out the local telephone directory, he was listed, so I called him up and visited with him several times. He had a job flying for someone and seemed happy.

Then, in the late 1970s after I had returned to Louisville, Lew called me out of the blue as he was travelling from his home up north to Huntsville, Alabama, where he said he was working on some major solar-power project. He arranged to stop by my office in Jeffersonville, Indiana, and we yakked for a few hours. After that, I heard that he had become involved in a scheme to search for and seize some gold that was hidden in an unidentified temple on the top of a mountain in the Peruvian Andes—in a helicopter. Whatever one thinks about Lew, I truly believe that he was a combination of genius, engineer, inventor, pilot and storyteller.

That was the last information I received about Lew's unusual activities until the early 1980s, when I heard that he had died.

Lew Whinnery was quite a character, and a hell of a pilot, too. Most importantly, he taught me so much about flying in the bush—what it takes to be a backcountry pilot, using short runways and rough fields for takeoffs and landings in the wild. From him, I learned important lessons about flying by instinct, or by the seat of your pants. We were more like the aviators of the 1920s and '30s who flew without weather forecasts, navigational aids, flight plans or control towers. In plain words, you were on your own. Make it or break it.

§

Let's move on from Lew to a more famous public figure.

Quite often, the British Royal Navy would carry some monarch or another to make an official visit to the Turks and Caicos. The last such visit, just prior to my arrival in the Islands, had been in 1966, when Queen Elizabeth herself stopped by. Ann Dempsey told me that she not only met Her Royal Majesty, but she had lunch with her aboard the Royal Yacht *Brittania*.

However, the high point of the social season in 1973 occurred as the result of a visit by none other than Charles,

Prince of Wales! That year, Prince Charles was one of the crew when HMS *Minerva* was making its Island rounds; indeed, he visited both Grand Turk and South Caicos.

"Lt. Windsor, Prince Charles" was a pleasant guy to hang out with—as I did one evening, courtesy of my British friends Robin and Sheila Laing. Hosting a dinner party to honor the Prince, they invited about a dozen people, including Bob and Bonnie Rowley and us. We heard that some of the British ex-pats on the Island were a bit miffed because they weren't invited. But it was Robin and Sheila's guest list to invite as they wished.

In any event, Noreen and I became engaged in a stimulating discussion with Prince Charles about scuba diving. It seems that he had been diving nearby and stepped on a sea urchin, receiving a painful wound on his foot from the spiny creature. As he mentioned that misstep, Bob Rowley, who had a few drinks and was starting to get sloshed, advised the Prince, "Piss on your foot when that happens, it'll heal it quickly." Fortunately, Bonnie quickly guided Bob away before any other inappropriate—albeit humorous—comments could be made.

There were no women on the Prince's ship, and I think he enjoyed the company of assorted locals and diverse guests when he left the vessel for parties and dinners. In fact, during his stay, he played in a couple of cricket matches for the HMS *Minerva* team as it competed against the locals. Unfortunately for him, records from the T & C National Museum show that his first innings was short: Maurice Hanchell bowled him out first ball and the Navy team went onto defeat. In South Caicos, Norman Saunders' Cockburn Harbour Cricket Club also beat the Royal Navy team, with the Prince making 12 runs this time. Congratulations if you understand cricket. I prefer baseball.

Chapter 9: The Adventures of Ton Ton

"Haiti is a place of great potential—and always will be."
—Anonymous

Another character in my island story deserves a chapter of his own. Let me tell you about an extraordinary fellow named Ton Ton, who had run away from his native Haiti to the Bahamas, and ended up in Georgetown, Exuma. There, Ton Ton, who was maybe 5-10 years younger than me, became familiar with all the personnel from Provident, Ltd., serving as sort of a jack of all trades for us.

Speaking French, Ton Ton had a terrible stutter; his broken English was even worse—it was really useless. Ditto with the Creole tongue, his preferred spoken language. However, he seemed to always understand the basics of whatever Fritz Ludington told him to do; so, he used to wash cars, clean up around the Two Turtles Inn and perform whatever odd jobs he was assigned.

During one 4th of July vacation interval, when Teddy Roosevelt, Kippy DuPont and a bunch of the partners and other friends had come down to the Islands, we had purchased a huge quantity of gigantic explosives for a homegrown fireworks show. Fritz directed Ton Ton to dig a large, deep hole in the rear of the Two Turtles so that we could place the skyrockets, mortars and other explosives in it for safekeeping until we could ignite them later. Then we all went off drinking, with no one giving a second thought about Ton Ton and his project. Well, Ton Ton dug, and dug and dug; when we eventually returned and discovered him, he was seven feet down, with water pouring in on him because he was down to sea level! And he just kept digging. That was Ton Ton.

Inevitably, there came a day when Ton Ton was snatched up by the Bahamian police and deported to Haiti. We merely said, "Well, that's the end of Ton Ton." Well, no such luck. A year later, I was just standing around out at the South Caicos airport, watching a big Bahamas Airways Avro 748 come in, which was always the big excitement of the week. The 748 was a powerful, medium-sized turboprop airliner designed by the British in the late 1950s as a replacement for the aging DC-3s. The first passenger down the ramp was a black man who looked somewhat familiar. The gentleman then saw me, ran over, grabbed me and gave me a hug, saying "C-C-Cap'n Em-Em-Embry!" Needless to say, it was Ton Ton.

The immigration and customs agents immediately started looking at me, asking, "Does this guy have a passport?" They believed that he was a Haitian, and they were pretty sure that he didn't have permission to be where he was. How he returned to the Bahamas, then boarded a Bahamas Airways flight to South Caicos, nobody will ever know, because Ton Ton could never adequately explain it. But it happened. That was Ton Ton.

In any event, I assured the authorities that he was a close friend of Fritz Ludington's and mine, and that we would certainly stand good for him, because he had come down to be the chief cook for the Third Turtle. At the time, this was really an inspired guess on my part, since I needed to figure out some excuse for keeping him in the country. So, the officials all put their heads together and concluded, "Oh, well, if Embry says it's okay, it must be okay." Quickly, I hustled Ton Ton into my airplane, flew him over to Provo, called Fritz on the way and declared, "I got an old buddy of yours here, you ought to come meet him," without identifying who it was. Tommy accompanied Fritz to the airport, and neither of them could believe it—the return of Ton Ton!

For his part, Ton Ton just went berserk in his own way when he saw Fritz, because he knew that the Boss would look after him. Fritz forever had a great soft spot in his heart for people who were just absolutely hopeless or in dire straits; he would take them in, feed, clothe and shelter them, and, even if they couldn't do damn thing and were obviously ineffective at work, he would keep them on the payroll. We ended up paying a lot of useless people that way. But to Fritz, it was the right thing to do.

By the way, that era in the West Indies was distinctly different from today: A lot of my colleagues and co-workers didn't have passports, although I did, and absolutely no one had a work permit from the government. Passports, ID's and government-required paperwork were just not that big of a deal back then. Hard to believe, but true.

Now, Fritz possessed the ability to impress everyone as being a real hard ass. Which in truth was not the case. The individuals who were capable of achieving something but skirted out of work were the ones whom he didn't care for. But if you were really and truly hopeless, bleak and despairing, then Fritz would lend a helping hand. Does that sound odd? I guess you can draw your own conclusions about him, one way or another.

After Ton Ton came to work at the Third Turtle, I mentioned to Fritz my conversation with the officials at South Caicos—that our Haitian friend was going to be the next great French chef in the Islands. Fritz replied, "Well, what the hell, put him in the kitchen." As it turned out, Ton Ton turned out to be a pretty darn good cook; so much so, that he worked successfully in the kitchen for years.

We eventually learned that, in addition to his culinary expertise, Ton Ton had learned to play the guitar—and carry a tune—somewhere in his travels; he knew quite a few songs in Creole and French. The first evening that he played and sang, everyone enjoyed it, but no one really paid any attention to the significance of his performance. Finally, we all felt stupid upon realizing that when he sang, he didn't stutter! In his ordinary speech, he stuttered horribly in Creole, French and English, but as a singer, his stammering disappeared and his serenading was quite pleasant and on key.

A brief digression about music: The Turks and Caicos Islanders were famous for their rake-and-scrape bands, featuring the use of the handsaw as their main instrument, along with the box guitar, concertina, triangle, accordion and various kinds of drums. The saw was played by scraping an object, usually an old knife blade, along the saw's teeth. Its popularity eventually spread to the Bahamas and other nearby islands, where it was called ripsaw music. One of the most popular groups was Goo and the Silver Saw, which performed at places we regularly patronized.

Islander Oswaldo Ariza remembered: "Everything happened on Pond Street. There was a social place where all the government people from England would find themselves at night. The entertainment before then was the ripsaw, which was nice and authentic. The musicians made the drum out of goat or cow skin. When it got dull, during intermission they would light the fire and heat the drum." Many times, I saw those drums being heated to shrink the skins.

As I mentioned earlier, quite a few people were involved in helping to unload the salvageable items from the *Anna*, Bob Kellogg's vessel, after it ran aground about 100 yards offshore in Sapodilla Bay off Providenciales. It was basically an all-hands-on-deck operation, and it was a difficult and involved effort. Ton Ton was included in the work.

After a couple of days of being left behind to keep watch at the dock, he convinced us to let him row a little Boston Whaler out to the *Anna*. First manufactured in 1958, Boston Whaler boats were very stable, had great carrying capacity and were basically indestructible. Those two features, along with great performance and rough weather handling, made them very desirable and seaworthy vessels. Also, since the Whaler was so light in weight compared to the other boats at the time, it could be propelled by lower-horsepower engines. Whalers are still advertised and marketed as "The Unsinkable Legend." I believe that the one he took, a 13-foot skiff, had serial number 50, meaning it was the 50th one produced by the Boston Whaler company. You probably already know what's going to happen.

Well, Ton Ton took the Whaler out to the *Anna* with instructions to start the pump and drain the water out of the ship. A pretty simple job, but he managed to screw it up, losing the oars or the engine or something in the process. We figured this out the next day when someone cruised out to investigate how the Haitian was getting along, and found no Ton Ton, no Boston Whaler and the *Anna* resting on the bottom again.

Although most of the *Anna* was still visible—it was in a shallow resting place—everyone was swearing and cursing, "God damn Ton Ton," and speculating about where he was. Then, after a while, Ton Ton had still not appeared, and we were all becoming slightly worried about his whereabouts, or his fate. In addition, the other guys in the Third Turtle kitchen were really becoming pissed off because he wasn't there to perform his cooking duties. We finally concluded that, because both Ton Ton and the Boston Whaler were missing, maybe he was indeed lost or in serious trouble on the high seas.

So, we started a search effort for him. Fritz took his plane and flew around for a lengthy time over the west coast of Providenciales—where the wind might have driven the Haitian—and then over to West Caicos. Fritz's frantic search yielded no clues and no Ton Ton.

Finally, just on an off chance, Fritz flew another 30 miles to Little Inagua and made a pass flying low over the beach. Sure enough, there was Ton Ton dashing up and down the beach and waving his arms madly at the plane. A relieved Fritz radioed back to us and reported, "Well, found him—on Little Inagua. Somebody go get him." Inagua is the southernmost district of the Bahamas, comprising the islands of Great Inagua, where Morton Salt Company formerly had a huge operation for many years, and Little Inagua. I don't know if the early Boston Whaler was ever recovered—it still may be floating around somewhere, unsinkable to the last.

Someone took a boat out from Great Inagua and picked up our Haitian fellow. Poor Ton Ton was scared to death. Why? He was the only human being on the island—a herd of wild donkeys were the only other living things he encountered, and their antics and running-romps just terrorized him. Those donkeys probably scared the bejeezus out of him when they ran at him and startled him in the middle of the night as he was starving to death, out of water and dehydrated. Plus, he had no idea of his geographic location because he was an uneducated, bush-born Haitian. Maybe he was lucky he didn't encounter any of the wild goats there. They would have finished him for sure. In any event, someone from Inagua picked him up in a boat and took him back there, where once again—for the second time—he boarded a Bahamas Airways flight that deposited him in South Caicos.

Yelling "Cap'n Embry!" and looking like holy hell, Ton Ton sprinted off the airplane straight into my waiting arms. He was sunburned all over, peeling, salt-encrusted and starving—a poor, miserable fellow. In that instant, a grand idea came to me—I gathered him up, and off we went, home to Noreen.

In matters out of the ordinary, Noreen tended to be calm, cool and collected—you just couldn't surprise her with any turn of events. In like manner, she was totally unflappable when I walked through the door with Ton Ton. I could have brought a baby elephant home with me and said, "Noreen, we have to take care of this elephant," and she would have replied, "Okay, then we will take care of the elephant." And that's the way it was when I arrived with

Ton Ton. I said, "Noreen, here's Ton Ton, the poor fellow is in bad shape." Already familiar with him from the Third Turtle, she took stock of his condition and immediately started calming and comforting him, saying, "Oh, poor Ton Ton, poor Ton Ton."

Then began the task of putting Ton Ton back in working order. After re-hydrating him with plenty of water, we provided him with a shower, then mustered up food for a little meal for him and put him to bed—whereupon he slept for about 18 hours. My God, he was tough and just had a natural resilience to the hardships the world had given him. Staying with us for a day or so, he continued to mend and improve. Meanwhile, most of the people of South Caicos thought Noreen and I were quite mad—boarding and caring for this strange Haitian fellow who couldn't talk straight. Eventually, with sufficient rest and recovery, he returned to his cooking responsibilities at the Third Turtle, where he continued to refine his cooking competence.

Upon leaving the Islands in 1976, I lost track of Ton Ton and don't know whatever became of him. However, I carry many fond memories of his relationship and interaction with all of us in the Turks and Caicos and Bahamas. He was OK.

Chapter 10: Baggage Boy to General Manager

"Keep thy airspeed up, lest the earth
come from below and smite thee."
—William Kershner

Eventually, the outfit for which I was flying, Air Caicos, went broke—the airline just had too many seats and too few passengers; plus, the requested route approvals to Miami did not materialize as expected. Being out of work was quite a devastating experience for Noreen and me because we had just built a house on Grand Turk, and Noreen had given birth to our first child, a brand new wonderful baby girl named Siofra, the cutest thing in the world. So, we had a newborn in a new house, and all of a sudden, a bankrupt employer and no job. In the Islands, there was no unemployment compensation, no welfare and no government support of any kind if you were out of work, especially if you're a foreigner—you were just flat out of luck.

In February 1972, shortly after my being laid off, Out Island Airways from Nassau, Bahamas took over the flying routes that Air Caicos served, and I spoke to these new airline folks, hoping that they would hire me as a pilot. No such luck. They told me that they had brought their own contingent of pilots from Nassau. However, they advised me that, although they had no current openings for pilots, if I wanted to work as a baggage boy, they would hire me for $50 a week. Well, fifty dollars was better than no dollars, so I went to work for my new employer doing the humble task of loading and unloading luggage, suitcases and other baggage.

As word got around about my new job, my local Island friends must have contacted Out Island Airways and complained about my treatment or pointed out to them that I had been regularly flying their very same scheduled routes for some time, saying, "Look now, we been use to having Captain Embry around, he's a fine pilot, why don't you give him a job?" So Out Island did so—after about a month—and I was back to making a salary that would adequately pay for our house, food and baby supplies. Thank goodness, I was flying again!

Within a fairly brief period after I was back in the air, Mr. Sherlock Hackley (1910-1992) and some other corporate-type gentlemen ventured down from Nassau to look around. Mr. Hackley had retired from Kaiser and was one of the principal owners of Out Island Airways. When they arrived, I was led to believe that these men just wanted to talk about the Islands and shoot the breeze. So, talk we did, and we had a pleasurable, enjoyable time together. Too dumb to figure it out at the time, I later realized that the whole process of meeting with me was really a lengthy and comprehensive job interview.

Evidently, they were looking at two candidates to be the General Manager of the new Turks and Caicos Airways—my friend Berkeley Baron and me. It is likely that what secured it for yours truly was the question that Mr. Hackley posed to both of us: "What is the most important thing about running an airline?" Berkeley replied, "To produce a safe and effective transportation system for the islanders." My response, designed because of a business economics course I had in college, was, "To make money for the stockholders." My answer won, and I got the job as GM of the airline, after being hired as its baggage boy only three months earlier.

One of the interesting people that Hackley brought with him was his accountant, Jorge Cardenas, from a well-to-do Cuban family, prior to the takeover by Fidel Castro. Jorge was a very considerate and personable guy, and we became friends. In addition to him, Hackley had some other Cuban connections, because his wife Helena had Cuban parentage; she had suffered significant real and personal property losses in Havana after the Cuban Communist revolutionaries took control.

Quickly I began my work as corporate chief of an airline with a total of five employees. For the flights on our newly-christened Turks and Caicos Airways, our fleet included Britten-Norman Islanders, twin-engine English airplanes that would carry a pilot plus nine passengers. The Model BN-2A-6 was really a great, rugged little plane with fixed landing gear. First designed produced in the mid-to-late 1960s, this light utility aircraft, regional airliner and cargo aircraft was one of the best-selling commercial aircraft types produced in Europe. Many are still in service with commercial operators around the world, and it is also utilized by the British Army and police forces in the United Kingdom.

More favorably for the profit-loss column, these Islanders only burned about 20 gallons of fuel per hour, as opposed to the 100 gallons per hour consumption of the DC-3s that we had flown for Air Caicos.

Out Island also employed a Trislander in its fleet. In comparison with the Islander, the BN-2A-Mk III Mark 3 Trislander had a stretched fuselage; strengthened, fixed tricycle landing gear; and, a third engine on the fuselage center line atop the fin. That third engine made it an odd-looking plane to the average onlooker. The Trislander had exceptional low-speed handling, extended endurance, increased payload, low noise and economical operating costs. Capable of taking off from a landing strip only 492 yards long, the Trislander could easily operate from unprepared or rough surfaces—perfect for us. Long and narrow, the plane could fit nine rows of seats; however, it had to be loaded extremely carefully, because the tail would tend to drop to the ground if overloaded to the rear.

These Islanders and Trislanders operated on an excellent, tight, twice-daily schedule between all the islands—Grand Turk, Salt Cay, South Caicos, Middle Caicos, North Caicos, Pine Cay, Providenciales—and then back again. We flew two complete trips through the entire Island chain every day—one in the morning, one in the evening—and then we would throw in a couple of mid-day trips to Salt Cay and South Caicos. Salt Cay was added because it was only 8 miles away, and South Caicos was included because there was more demand for traffic there. The bottom line was favorable: We were operating very economically with excellent passenger loads, in addition to assistance by a crew of first-rate mechanics.

A blond-haired, blue-eyed Jamaican named David Dumont was one of these proficient mechanics. Hearing him speak with your back turned to him, you would absolutely believe that he was black; then, you would turn around and see this white guy talking just like all the other Jamaicans. He was the youngest of six or seven boys, and his mother had kept him home from school until he was nine or ten years old because he was such a pleasant, sociable lad. He spent much of his early childhood playing by the docks, where his mother would watch him from her window and know that all was right with the world. It was easy for her to spot him because he was the only white-skinned boy there.

One of the pilots working for us was Bob Rowley, whom I had met in Providenciales where he refueled while ferrying an airplane to Puerto Rico or similar destination. Bob, a Massachusetts native, was my age; he had joined the U.S. Navy as a submariner immediately after graduating from high school. He had also flown for some New England outfit, patrolling the ocean, spotting and observing large schools of fish for the commercial fishing industry. Even today, large seiner vessels still use spotter planes to assist them in their fishing efforts.

After I became General Manager, I once flew a chartered flight down to Jamaica, and I ran into Bob at the airport in Kingston. He commented to me, "You know, we got a pretty good deal down here in Jamaica, Embry. If you want a job, why don't you come down here and I'll see that you get a pilot's job in Jamaica." My reply was, "Well, I dunno, Bob, we got a pretty good deal up at Turks and Caicos. If YOU want a job, come up there and I can guarantee you one with our airline." Sure enough, a few weeks later, he called and asked, "Are you serious about that job at Turks?" I responded, "Yeah." So, he came up and scrutinized the Airways situation; then, more importantly, he sent his wife Bonnie to look around, and she inspected the Island with an eye toward relocating. Evidently, she found it to her liking because he decided to take my job offer, and they both really settled in well.

Bob and Bonnie were both likeable people, and they became friends to Noreen and me. Eventually, Bob became Chief Pilot, my second-in-command who handled pilot qualifications and training. It all went to prove that we were operating a very worthy and efficient—albeit small—air service, with flights almost always on time.

After he left Turks and Caicos, Bob Rowley went on to work as a helicopter pilot and as sort of an undercover agent. With all his experience, he was so knowledgeable about the smuggling trade that the government used his skills to root out drug dealers and other smugglers. He lives in Key West, Florida now; around 2012, I had a good visit with him.

In addition to the rock-solid Bob Rowley-types, there were some unusual job seekers who dropped into our offices on Grand Turk, wanting to fly for us. One former 707 Captain for East African and Ugandan Airways arrived from England in a 35-foot sloop looking for a pilot's position. He filled in for a short while, then was off again in his sailboat to parts unknown.

Along the way, I often thought how boring it must have been to work as a pilot for Eastern Airlines—flying that shuttle from Washington to New York, back and forth and back again, day after day after day.

Eventually, the personnel at Turks and Caicos Airways—and later at Haiti Air Inter—took on the look of the United Nations. We had almost as many nationalities as staffers. They were American, Canadian, English, Swiss, German, Belgian Congolese, Jamaican, Haitian, a Laplander from Finland (that pilot didn't work out so well) and of course, Turks and Caicos Islanders. Quite an international crew.

In 1972, while in charge of Turks and Caicos Airways, I did something that resonates around the world even to this day.

In air travel, the International Air Transport Association's location identifier is a unique 3-letter code, commonly known as IATA code, that is used to primarily identify locations of airports throughout the world. For example, the airline code for Atlanta is ATL; for Louisville is SDF; for Houston is HOU, and so forth. Well, except for Grand Turk (GDT) and South Caicos (XSC), the Turks and Caicos Islands lacked any such codes. I decided we needed more of them, and I developed additional codes.

So, even today, the following codes which I thought up are still in effect: NCA-North Caicos; MDS-Middle Caicos; PLS-Providenciales; SLX-Salt Cay.

Mr. Hackley provided many excellent opportunities for me to grow professionally in my General Manager position. He arranged for me to go to New York and spend some time learning from Alvin P. "Al" Adams, an aviation pioneer who was a former head of Western Airlines and Seaboard Airways and an executive at Pan American and Airbus. Adams was quite a guy, and that was an outstanding opportunity.

Then, in the mid-1970s, Mr. Hackley and I attended gatherings of the Conquistadores del Cielos—Conquerors of the Sky—where I met many aviation trailblazers and innovators, including former astronauts Frank Borman, later head of Eastern Airlines; Neil Armstrong, first man on the moon; and Bob Prescott, a World War II combat ace with the Flying Tigers in China, who also "flew the hump" and later founded the Flying Tiger Line, the first scheduled cargo airline in the United States.

Another unforgettable person I met at one of these gatherings was General Curtis LeMay, renowned Air Force leader in World War II, who as USAF Chief of Staff became the architect of America's strategic air power system. He was a brilliant man who told me that if you're in a war, you must shut your mind to its horrors and be willing to do anything it takes to win. In 1968, LeMay was George Wallace's running mate during his unsuccessful, anti-mainstream Independent Party presidential bid.

Jack G. Real, president of Hughes Aircraft Company, was another trendsetter I encountered at these gatherings. Jack was an important Howard Hughes confidante—he arranged for Hughes to be moved to the Bahamas in 1970. He was also past president of Hughes Helicopter and an aerospace pioneer who helped design the SR-71 Blackbird, a long-range, Mach 3+ strategic reconnaissance aircraft operated by the US Air Force. Plus, Jack was a first-rate gentleman to hang out with.

Al Adams, mentioned above, was a founder of Conquistadores del Cielo, founded in 1937, which was once described by the *New York Times* as a "shadowy all-male organization of top-level aviation executives whose continuing semi-annual conclaves in the rough are so secretive that it can only be assumed that when they get together at a western dude ranch they laugh themselves silly." That is all so true, at least from my own experience.

My boss Mr. Hackley was a permanent and regular associate of this aviation organization, due to his membership in the famed Bohemian Club of San Francisco. This Bohemian group was founded in 1872 and served as a gathering place for journalists, artists and musicians. It later developed a diverse membership of many local and global leaders, ranging from artists and musicians to businessmen and scientists.

Meetings of this heavy-duty airline group would take place twice a year at various locales. Once, we gathered in Wyoming at the A-Bar-A Ranch, owned by Charlie Gates, head of Gates Rubber Company and Learjet. Mr. Hackley and I flew there on the General Electric corporate jet, courtesy of Jack Steele Parker, Vice Chairman and Executive Officer of that company from 1968 to 1980, who himself had an award-winning background in aeronautics. Another time, we went to the Grand Hotel in Fairhope, Alabama on Mobile Bay for a similar gathering.

It was certainly fun and interesting to hang out with the heads of various airlines from around the world: American, United, Eastern, Pan Am, BOAC, SAS and Hughes Air West, just to name a few. As for me, I was the Vice President and General Manager of the Turks and Caicos Airways, a guest of member Sherlock Hackley of Out Island Airways. Sometimes they all dressed as conquistadors and cavorted in various fun activities. Needless to say, I learned a lot from these fellows as we threw knives, cast plugs and competed in target shooting and other contests and diversions. Later, when I was looking for a job, I wrote to many of them in hopes that their memory of me would generate an employment opportunity.

Speaking of airline executives, I had an interesting connection with Ms. Jean Rich, founder of Miami-based Rich International Airways. One of the first women to own and manage an airline, she began her corporate livelihood by carrying cargo with a single C-46 in 1970; later, she expanded by promoting chartered flights throughout the Caribbean and West Indies.

Did I ever meet her? No, but I did help her once in an emergency of sorts. One of her C-46s was stuck once on Grand Turk when its starter motor went out on a run to Haiti; at that time, the prognosis for such a malfunction was typically countless days of delay.

Having pity on the pilot, I came to the rescue, so to speak, and offered to start it. My plan was to rope-start it by tying a ¾ inch rope around the propeller, attach that line to a truck and give it a rapid pull while directing the pilot to flip the ignition on—just like pulling the cord on a boat's outboard motor. I executed my plan to perfection, and it started!

Figuring that I had saved her a great deal of money and down-time for an important cargo plane in her fleet, I promptly sent Ms. Rich a bill for $700.00, which she never paid. Not a cent, not a reply. She had a reputation for being cheap, she proved it, and I just let the matter drop.

Coincidentally many years later, on a hunting trip to Zimbabwe, I flew on Zambian Airways, also known as Zambian Scareways. Somehow, we were shunted onto a Rich Airways Boeing 707 charter flight that was extremely full. After a brief meeting and conversation with the pilot and co-pilot, I learned that it was necessary for them to make an unplanned landing to refuel. However, when we made our final approach to land in the West African city of Banjul, the capital of The Gambia, no lights or directional aids had been turned on the runway, because no one at the airfield knew in advance that we were arriving. What a way to run an airline! Finally, in 1997, after a long history of financial and maintenance deficiencies, Rich Airways went bankrupt, closed shop and was disbanded.

Some airline administrators had lengthier resumes and more high-level connections, but my hands-on work as a bush pilot-mechanic-general manager gave me both a pilot's skills and an executive's business sense. My flying experiences and lessons about island life took me where

I wanted to be. I felt satisfied—and ready for my next challenge.

Chapter 11: Baby Doc, Voodoo & Howard Hughes

"Haiti is the graveyard of development projects." —Paul Farmer

Since we were successfully operating a few charters into Haiti, we decided to increase the number of scheduled flights into that country. When Fritz and I first flew to Haiti, "President for Life" Francois "Papa Doc" Duvalier was still in power; after his death in April 1971, his son Jean-Claude "Baby Doc" Duvalier, then 19 years old, assumed power as President.

Haiti occupies one third of Hispaniola, with its neighbor to the east, the Dominican Republic (DR), situated on the remainder. It's only about a hundred miles from Haiti to Turks and Caicos—a 45-50-minute plane flight—and a significant amount of trading had always taken place between them, primarily on locally-made sailing sloops.

Compared to Turks and Caicos, I always found Haiti to be more hot and humid. It seemed to me that Villarosa, the grand mansion that I will discuss later, always had an agreeable breeze, probably because it was located on a tall hill in Port-au-Prince, the capital. But nowhere else could I find relief.

With no fanfare, Turks and Caicos Airways opened for business in Port-au-Prince. The downtown office out of which we operated the airline had no windows, but it did have air conditioning, which was rare for that city. Our building looked like it was originally an alley that someone roofed over to enclose it. Not only was it plain-looking and austere, but it also lacked plumbing. Imagine that! The sign that hung outside simply said, "Turks and Caicos Airways."

During the time that I was flying charters from Port-au-Prince to Santo Domingo, I once had the occasion to meet the son of the former private secretary of Juan Peron, the iconic, charismatic, three-time President of Argentina. When I met this gentleman, he was working for the Dominican Republic government; a charming fellow, he had moved there from Argentina. Typically, it was dangerous for South American political leaders and their families to stay in one place too long in those days, or their political rivals would catch up with them.

During several past trips to Haiti, I had become acquainted with Marc "Butch" Ashton, and we developed a good friendship. Butch was an American citizen who had lived in Haiti all his life; he spoke perfect Creole, French and English. He had married a very beautiful local woman, Myriam, who came from a Cuban-French-Haitian family. The primary business that he operated was ABC Tours, a travel agency in Port-au-Prince. Personally close to the Duvaliers, he knew Baby Doc well—which was basically a Get Out of Jail Free card in Haiti.

Since I was so close to the Ashtons, let me digress a moment to talk about Butch's father, Horace.

Mr. Horace Dade Ashton (1883-1976) had a fascinating history: He had served as the personal photographer for Teddy Roosevelt and had taken photos of the early Wright Brothers airplane flights. He had been an explorer in the 1920s, roaming the North African desert, Tibet, China, Japan and other fascinating places, continually studying world religions. In addition, he was an aviator in the early days of flying—perhaps being the first flyer to loop the Brooklyn Bridge!

In the 1930s, Horace Ashton was stationed in Yugoslavia, where he met King Peter's cousin, a beautiful and charming young lady from Dubrovnik, at a Royal Ball. It was love at first sight, as they say; he informed the Royal dame that he was madly in love with her, that he was going back to the United States to divorce his wife and then return to marry her. Quite a plan, and she never gave such trifling talk another thought. But, sure enough, a few months later Mr. Ashton returned to Yugoslavia, final divorce decree in hand, and he formally proposed marriage. The young lady accepted and later became Madame Gordana Ashton.

In 1939, the United States needed a cultural attaché to the U.S. Embassy in Haiti; due to Horace Ashton's extensive knowledge of the island since his first visit there in 1906, and the Voodoo—or Vodou—religion, he received the appointment. He chose to be there in light of the fascination with religion that he had developed during his world travels, especially in Africa. In any event, he and his wife ended up at the American Embassy in Port-au-Prince; the residence they occupied since 1953 was known as Villarosa, located on a tall hill overlooking the Presidential Palace. On the cover of the book by Butch Ashton that I mention later, there is a wonderful painting by Horace Ashton of the porch at Villarosa. Occasionally I would stay at that huge, marvelous residence; there were three extra rooms at Villarosa that were set aside for pilots in a type of bed-and-breakfast arrangement. They had plenty of staff to help Gordana, who was in charge.

Now, there's an old saying that Haiti is 90% Catholic and 100% Voodoo, and there's much truth to that. Somehow, Horace Ashton from Virginia had established and cultivated an interest in the religious practice of Voodoo, and he became the only white Voodoo priest in Haiti. In fact, he was dubbed "Houngan Blanc," meaning the white priest. Suffice it to say that Mr. Ashton was very serious about practicing these rites.

From my own personal experiences, I would never label Voodoo as being fake or bogus. I saw and heard too much that demonstrated otherwise. For example: People would mention to me how their dear, departed relatives had appeared to them as the result of a Voodoo ceremony; or, it was verified that a Haitian woman had been fed a magic pill and worked as a zombie slave. Although the Voodoo priests often put on a show for curious observers, the genuine ceremonies were not open to outsiders or unbelievers. But it was not an evil religion by any means, or one that embraced wicked outcomes.

Mr. Ashton, the white priest, was a very fascinating old man. We attended a party to celebrate Horace's 90th birthday, and a younger, 50ish woman-friend of his who always acted very coquettishly approached him and asked, "Now, Horace, what would you like for your birthday?" Mr. Ashton looked at her and growled, "A piece of ass!" Of course, that brought the house down. He passed away shortly after we left the Islands.

Another amusing incident occurred in Haiti when Butch learned that I wanted a Haitian operator's license for identification purposes and to drive a motor vehicle. It was unnecessary for me to take any test—Butch was in charge. He dispatched someone to obtain a photo from me for the license. His courier later came back with a license that identified me as "Embry Lucker," with black hair, black eyes and far, far shorter than I really was. Oh, well, it didn't really matter, because the average Haitian policeman couldn't read anyway.

A political associate of Butch's who became a social friend of Noreen and mine was an interesting character named Auguste "Tipouche" Duyon, who happened to be Baby Doc's personal private secretary. While we were in Haiti, an incident occurred involving Tipouche which provided us an interesting and revealing view of life in the Third World and in the world of dictatorships.

Butch owned a little place on the beach that he and his wife Myriam used as a getaway resort on the weekends; it was two hours out of Port-au-Prince. To reach it, you had to drive along Haiti's sharply-indented west coast through Duvalierville, which was partly built and improved in 1962 by President-for-Life Francois Duvalier as a monument to his own generosity and kindness. In 1986, never having become the grand metropolis that Duvalier hoped, it changed its name back to its original Cabaret, some 28 years after the Duvalier dynasty was toppled.

On one occasion, David Dumont; Bob Rowley and his wife Bonnie; Tipouche and his girlfriend; Butch's brother-in-law; and Noreen and I were all staying at the beach retreat. Several of the guests attended a dance at a local village that was accessible only by a narrow road along the coastline. It was during the return trip that the adventure began.

Tipouche, who had a broken leg encased in a heavy plaster cast at the time, was driving home— "He had drink taken," as the Irish say—and his girlfriend was in the passenger seat. Butch, accompanied by David and Bob, was following Tipouche home when the lead car suddenly swerved off the road right into the ocean.

Butch quickly pulled over to the side of the road, and David and Bob stripped and jumped in to successfully save Tipouche and his lady friend, although the former had some difficulty escaping the car. After regaining his breath and wits, Tipouche informed his rescuers that they were not finished—he needed a briefcase that was in the trunk of the car, plus he wanted the license plate taken off the car to avoid unwanted publicity. Surprisingly, David and Bob carried out his directions without complaint.

All then travelled back to Butch's resort without further incident. Once there, the briefcase was opened to dry out, whereupon the ladies observed that it contained a pistol, two or three passports and many stacks of U.S. $100 bills. Bonnie and Noreen were very surprised at this, but not Myriam. She knew that was Tipouche's emergency stash—his getaway kit. It was likely that he returned to the presidential palace on the following Monday, kept his job and was issued a new car. I have no idea how he reported the loss of the vehicle. That's the way things worked out for friends of Papa Doc and Baby Doc, and that was typical of Haiti.

One truth apparent to me was that Haitian politics could be described as an impenetrable mystery grounded in self-interest. Assorted factions within the country were constantly plotting to overthrow the current regime. Once, Butch, Myriam, Gordana and a couple of the layover pilots and I sat on the porch of Villarosa watching a Haitian Coast Guard ship shell the palace in an unsuccessful coup attempt—it was just plain laughable.

Now, let me tell you how we assisted Butch, and, in doing so, eventually benefitted from his government connections.

In the spring of 1969, a group of Haitian exiles with a big Connie—a Lockheed Constellation airliner—had appeared on South Caicos. Looking paramilitary in various types of uniforms, they had been skulking around and acting very secretively for several weeks. Most of us determined that this group was planning to invade Haiti, at that time ruled by Papa Doc Duvalier, widely known as a repressive dictator.

One of these furtive fellows and I engaged in an interesting conversation one day. As we talked, he was acting highly secretively, continually casting glances over his shoulder as if someone else was watching or listening. Finally, he asked me, "Do you want to make a lot of money?" Of course, my reply was, "Sure." He then said, "Well, we're planning an invasion of Haiti." I responded, "Yeah, I figured it out." He then excitedly asked, "How, how, how?" At that point I explained to him, "It's a fairly unusual occurrence for a bunch of Haitians with a large cargo plane 100 miles off the coast of Haiti to be hanging around looking and acting slyly and secretly."

Eventually, this self-described General proposed a deal to me: If I would allow the use of our aircraft in an invasion of Haiti, and if their takeover was successful, he would give me $10,000 and make me a Colonel in the Haitian Air Force. At that time, there was a real Haitian Air Force that consisted of DC-3s and P-51 Mustangs from World War II. I knew Colonel Danache who was a member of that Haitian flying corps. Later, in 1995, after years of military interference in politics, including dozens of military coups, Haiti disbanded its military.

Anyway, because I thought this bunch was on the incompetent side, that money and promotion really didn't sound like a good offer to me. So, I put the guy off for a while, and I called my friend Butch in Port-au-Prince, informing him all about what was happening. My thinking was that Butch, armed with this information, could make some special goodwill for himself with the regime. Although it turned out that Papa Doc's people already knew what was going on with this bunch of invaders, they just didn't know specifically what was going to happen, or when.

In any event, these poor, stupid Haitian exiles took off one day in their "bomber" and bombarded Port-au-Prince near Papa Doc's Presidential Palace. The bombs consisted of 55-gallon drums of aviation fuel that were pushed out of the plane's cargo door in the hope that they would explode upon hitting the ground. The net result of the whole bombing and invasion scheme? One unfortunate Haitian soldier was crushed by a falling fuel barrel; and, all the insurance companies declared that their policies were invalid that day because so many people were excitedly speeding along the streets, driving into shop windows and crashing into each other—all these accidents due to the threat of bombs and invasion. What a fiasco.

Other than that one casualty, the bombing run was a total failure, and the rebel plane limped into Freeport in the Bahamas; there, all the poor sods who participated were arrested and turned over to the authorities in Miami for aiding and abetting the overthrow of a friendly foreign power or some such violation. In any event, after that failed coup, Butch Ashton was very friendly to us since our information allowed him to significantly increase his influence with the Duvalier government—and that meant that our airline also benefited. In fact, that's how we obtained permission to run regularly scheduled flights into Cap-Haïtien and Port-au-Prince.

You see, not long after that incident, Sherlock Hackley, Butch and I hatched a plan to schedule a local flight connecting those two main Haitian cities. They were only 30 minutes apart by air, but an astounding 8 or 9 hours apart by motor vehicle, mainly due to the horrendous state of the roads. After researching the local maps and scouting a number of smaller towns with landing fields, we also decided to schedule flights into Cap-Haïtien, Port-au-Prince, Jacmel, Jeremie, Las Cayes and Port-de-Paix. The Haitian Air Force had been flying on these routes, but on a very irregular and unscheduled basis, as only they could do.

The meeting that we had one morning with Dr. Serge Fourcand, the Minister of Commerce and Industry, was fascinating. That ministry is an important presidential cabinet-level position in Haiti. Obviously, we needed an official license from the government to operate the airline schedule that we were instituting. We advised Fourcand that, if our venture was successful, we would create a Haitian company, and the venture would become all-Haitian-operated in the future. In plain words, we would work ourselves out of a job project if we were successful. Perhaps this idea of training Haitians to take over was more of a hope than a certain thing, but we were absolutely sincere about making it work.

Initially, the Minister was very skeptical about the entire proposal, telling us that Air France already had been planning for some time to set up an airline to serve the Haitian interior. Fourcand stressed that the French airline company was well established and quite important, that they had studied all the issues extensively and that they would probably, in six months or so, begin such an airline service. My response was to agree that Air France was a major, successful international airline, but that we could provide this service just as well, maybe better, since we were used to operating a small airline with modest numbers of passengers.

Fourcand acted strongly unconvinced about us and our chances, but perhaps Baby Doc had informed him that Butch Ashton was a friend of his, and that we had assisted Butch, who was mentoring our proposal. I certainly believe that to be the case.

In any event, he continued paying attention to my sales pitch and then asked, "When would you plan on starting this airline of yours?" I replied, "Tomorrow morning would be fine." Somewhat taken aback, he responded by saying, "Alright, if you think that you can begin a scheduled airline by tomorrow morning, you have my permission—go right ahead then." Fourcand even approved an agreed fare schedule at that time.

The Haitians obviously thought that we were stupid and had no way of implementing service so quickly, but I had previously planned for such an eventuality; all of the pilots, aircraft mechanics and other personnel that we needed were already lined up and waiting. We had addressed all the operational details for a quick start. We were good to go.

After leaving the meeting, I made a few quick phone calls and, by the afternoon, everyone in Turks and Caicos whom we needed for the start-up had arrived in Port-au-Prince. We then placed announcements on local radio stations all over Haiti, established a counter relationship with the Pan American people at the airport—the station manager there was an older Haitian man who helped us out with our ticketing process—and by 7:00 the next morning, we kicked off our Haitian airline business with scheduled service to Cap-Haïtien!

Initially, one problem that we did encounter was that Haitians were quite used to everything on the island being late—Haitians being Haitians, nothing ever happened in a timely manner. So, for the first 3 or 4 weeks, even though passengers would book seats on a 7:00 AM flight or whatever time, they wouldn't show up until much later. The Haitians just assumed that, being a Haitian operation, we weren't going to be operating on time. However, the only way that we could successfully travel our circuit of local stops around the country was if we left on time, all the time.

My employees were panicking because we'd just be sitting there, waiting for everyone to show up. "What are we going to do?" they grumbled. My response was, "Don't worry, we'll just have our flights leave on time, even though we may have to fly with an empty plane. Hopefully, our Haitian passengers will get the idea that *we* always operate on time." That's all it took. They did figure out that we meant what we said, and that we absolutely meant to follow the posted schedule. Now, it did take some time for this to transpire, but eventually everyone caught on to the system, and it worked very effectively.

The plane that we used in this one-plane operation was a turboprop deHavilland Twin Otter, an 18-passenger Canadian product. We had a 99.3 dispatch reliability, meaning that the plane was ready to fly 99.3% of all scheduled flights. Although not very fast, the Twin Otter was a short-takeoff-and-landing utility aircraft. Its fixed tricycle landing gear and high rate of climb made it the perfect plane for our local island schedule.

Servicing the Twin Otter in Haiti was a Canadian, Michael O'Zarko, an outstanding mechanic who did all the maintenance at night and on Sundays when we didn't operate. Since we conducted the entire airline within the Republic of Haiti with only one aircraft, we couldn't afford any breakdowns. It appeared that the Haitian government,

Air France and the Haitian Air Force were all just waiting for us to fall on our faces.

Speaking of the government, everything in our airline venture went exceedingly well for some time; that is, until we began experiencing the usual, frequent hassles with Haitian officials. The main problem was turnover of their key people, such as M. Fourcand, the Commerce and Industry Minister who originally gave us permission to operate. Two months after that critical meeting, he had been replaced; then, the new Minister wanted to know what all these foreigners were doing flying around his country in their airplanes. So, it was necessary for us to meet with the new man and again explain the entire situation, just as if we were brand new. Once again, we secured his vital permission, which lasted for a few more months until HE was replaced. Again and again and again. One of the issues that we faced was that we were not large or powerful enough to dictate economic terms to Baby Doc as some of the sizable, more established corporate entities were.

Meanwhile, our fuel costs were steadily increasing, so we attempted to justify an increase in fares. That was a mistake. By that time, M. Fourcand was back in power as Minister of Commerce and Industry, and, instead of approving a much-needed increase, he issued a letter announcing that we were LOWERING our fares by 10%. Huh? Without even allowing us a chance to discuss this unilateral action, he released his announcement to the press and the radio stations. We heard about his decision on the radio and had only 24 hours' notice before the decrease went into effect.

Unhappy about his decision, we looked into making a complaint with the courts, because it was not a good idea to disobey the Haitian government on your own. However, we asked around and, after further investigation, figured out that the courts didn't quite work in the fair and impartial way we hoped for either. We ultimately concluded that M. Fourcand must have been receiving under-the-table payments from the Haitian Air Force, which wanted to see us go bankrupt.

So, we decided to sidestep him and go directly to the President, Baby Doc Duvalier. Butch Ashton, acting as our intermediary, talked to the President and straightened everything out. In fact, orders were issued that we were to be treated with all available help and courtesy because we were going to become the national airline of Haiti. With that pronouncement, the attitude of government officials toward us improved remarkably. Quite a reversal of fortune. It was good to be politically connected.

It was about this time that I took Jack Real up on his offer to contact him in Freeport, Bahamas. Jack, from Hughes AirWest, was one of the aviation powers that I had met in Wyoming at the A Bar A Ranch for the Conquistadores del Cielo gatherings. He was one of Howard Hughes' key right-hand men. Since 1971, anyone involved in aviation in the Hughes empire reported to Jack, and Jack reported to Mr. Hughes, the billionaire business tycoon, entrepreneur, investor, aviator, aerospace engineer, inventor, filmmaker, and philanthropist. Although he became an eccentric recluse, Hughes still had a reputation as one of the most financially successful individuals in the world. In one book, Hughes' cousin later said, "Indeed, Jack Real was Howard Hughes' last best friend." For 20 years, Jack was as close to Hughes as any man.

Well, Jack and I happened to become very friendly at the A Bar A Ranch. Telling me that he made frequent trips to the Bahamas, he invited me to visit him whenever I was in Freeport. I enjoyed Jack's company, so I took him up on his offer.

When I stopped in Freeport, on my way to Miami to meet with our accountants, Jack met me at the airport and took me to the Xanadu Princess Hotel. The Bahamas Princess Resort and Casino was huge, about a thousand acres, with pools and a casino, and located right next to the International Bazaar. The Bazaar was a popular shopping district containing over 100 shops and restaurants from around the world. In addition, there were about 10 large hotels and two casinos on the Island at that time.

Anyway, Jack took me into the hotel and tower through some back door; then we got into an elevator that took one key to open and another to operate, where we zipped to the tenth of its eleven floors. Surprisingly, I found quite a large number of various rooms situated there—not all bedrooms—and a great many people. Some were reading, some were weightlifting, and some were bodyguards, secretaries and various assistants. At some point, Jack indicated to me that almost all of them were Mormons. Later, I learned that Hughes' considerable business holdings were overseen by a small group unofficially dubbed The Mormon Mafia because of the many members of the Church of Latter-Day Saints on the committee.

Jack accompanied me to his apartment, where we yakked for a while; at the time, I was too polite to ask if, in fact, Mr. Hughes was upstairs on the top floor, maybe just 10 feet away from us. During our conversation, I noticed that my friend had two telephones on a table next to his chair. Later during my visit, Jack and I were up late one evening, yakking and drinking, when suddenly one of these phones rang. Jack answered it and said, "Yeah, yeah, yeah, I'll be right up, okay?" After hanging up, he turned to me and calmly advised, "I've got to go somewhere, and I may be back in an hour, but it may be eight hours, and it could be three days, so when you wake up in the morning, if I'm not around, just go down the hall, wake up one of the pilots and tell him you want to go to Miami." Quite strange, but, in my mind, it all tied in with the eccentricity of Howard Hughes, whom I believed to be the unknown caller. In any event, I was sure at the time that Howard Hughes was in fact living one floor above us in the hotel, but he didn't want anyone in the world know precisely where he was staying, so no one was admitting or denying that he was in Freeport.

Well, when I awoke in the morning, there was no Jack around. As instructed, I walked down the hall, knocked on a pilot's door, and stated, "Jack said you would take me to Miami." Replying "Yes, certainly," the pilot whisked me out to the airport where we hopped onto one of Mr. Hughes' private jets and off we went to Miami. Pretty snazzy service for a Turks and Caicos guy, I thought.

On another occasion when I visited Jack Real in Freeport and spent the night, a huge party was thrown for the players in a professional tennis tournament that the hotel was hosting. Also present were quite a few top executives from various Hughes organizations from around the world. One such person was from a Central American airline, with which Hughes evidently had a management contract. After conversing for some time, he asked me, "Hey, you speak Spanish?" After I replied in the negative, he said, "Well, I got this little airline in Costa Rica that I want somebody to run. Think you could learn Spanish quick?" My response was, "No, I'm trying to put together something else right now." He replied, "Oh, something with Jack, huh?" I answered yeah and he said yeah, okay, and that was the end of that.

Living in Haiti was quite an experience. The ordinary way of life there was just so frustrating that even Noreen—the most adaptable person—didn't care for it very much. Although I never got the hang of the Creole language, Noreen immediately learned it and became good at speaking it, which was most helpful in dealing with the locals. She had terrific language aptitude.

She was also at times excitable, and stubborn. On one occasion when she was driving right in front of the palace in Port-au-Prince, a beggar kid said "F__Y__" to her when she wouldn't give him any change. Noreen immediately threw the door open, jumped out and smacked him! When I later learned this story, I was also told that the palace guards who were watching thought it was extremely funny and started laughing. Another time, when she was showing my mother, who was visiting, the sights of Port-au-Prince, Noreen discovered that she had received an unjustified parking ticket from a money-making Haitian cop who had a No Parking sign on a rolling stand that he wheeled around to entrap foreign tourists! She immediately went to the police department and forcefully demanded that they rescind it. When they were reluctant to do so, she quickly started dropping names of important Haitians that we knew, and eventually the authorities filed the matter away.

Living in a large, very attractive house in the mountains in LaBoule—about three miles southeast of Port-au-Prince—we had four servants: a cook, a laundress, a maid for the children and the gardener. The latter is a story in itself.

This fellow kept coming around, pleading with Noreen to be our gardener. Claire, our cook, said that he looked like a dependable sort, so Noreen asked him, "How much?" He replied, "Ten dollars a month." When Noreen immediately replied, "Okay, ten dollars a month," the poor fellow was crushed. He would have been much happier if she argued him down to only eight dollars, because he would have felt like he had not asked for too little to begin with. When Noreen agreed right off the bat to $10, well, it just ruined him—after that, he was always trying to obtain something extra from us.

Eventually, the gardener negotiated an arrangement with Noreen that the cook would feed him lunch every day. The cook was agreeable to this plan, but she wasn't about to admit the dirty, filthy gardener into her clean kitchen, so he had to eat his meals on the back steps. That was the pecking order.

Noreen was astonished that anyone would work for only $10 a month, but in Haiti there was much poverty, and wages were miniscule. Our cook was paid $30 a month, our children's maid received $25 per month plus toting privileges—the right to take home prepared but unused leftover food or other household items—which were never outrageous. To earn his pay, the gardener kept the flowers in satisfactory condition, kept our shoes shined and washed the cars each morning. Noreen often observed that having servants in Haiti was like having four or five extra children—supervising them was sometimes more trouble and inconvenience than they were worth. However, we felt obligated to employ these impoverished people; in addition, we were actually paying our cook and maid a larger salary than the wealthy Haitians were paying, so I guess we were doing okay by our house's servants.

Speaking of the children, Embry was 2 years old and Siofra maybe 5 years old when our family moved to Haiti. We enrolled our daughter in a little Haitian nursery school for a while, but young Embry whined around saying that he really missed "Fafa," and asked why he couldn't go to nursery school too. It their policy that they wouldn't accept children unless they were toilet-trained or brought their maid along with them each day. So, we did the latter and sent Janine the nursemaid each day with little Embry so that she could change his diaper when necessary. Both the kids had a really enjoyable time there; Embry thought it was great fun to join his sister at school each day.

Butch Ashton's children were close in age to our two kids, and there were several Haitians nearby who had youngsters; so, there were always birthday parties and other kids' events that they could attend. Our stay in Haiti was no doubt tougher on Noreen than anyone else in our little family; by necessity, I was busy working all the time while she tended to all the domestic matters at home. Although the Haitians were very friendly to us, it is difficult to be the only foreigners at dinner parties, receptions and other events, both from a cultural point of view, and also because it was not easy to understand the language as quickly as the natives could speak it.

When we resided in the mountains in LaBoule, we took an interest in Voodoo, collecting and reading several books on that subject. It was practiced everywhere around us, and we just wanted to be more educated about it. In one of these volumes, Noreen found a listing that showed the symbols and designs that represented various loas, or Haitian Voodoo spirits. In Voodoo, the loas are not deities in and of themselves, but intermediaries between the Supreme Creator and humanity.

In any event, when she sewed curtains for the windows in our house, she embroidered all of them with loa symbols. Not only were these curtains very attractive from inside, but the local Haitians believed that we were obviously very big deals in the Voodoo world since we had the symbols of all the chief spirits in our house, which was also the largest one in the area. So, in addition to being the only foreigners for several miles around, we received all sorts of exalted respect for our Voodoo curtains.

On one memorable spring evening, we witnessed the season's final rah-rah gala, sort of a combination of a Voodoo and Christian Lenten celebration. The rah-rah season basically corresponds to the season of Lent. These ceremonial gatherings can grow quite large, and the priests and participants are clothed in full costume, including masks, headdresses and various disguises.

It seemed as if everyone in the area turned out for this one—in front of our house, there were approximately 100 Haitians waving torches, cracking whips, singing and shouting. The drums they beat went, "Boom, Boom, Boom!" and they were answered by drums from over the mountain, going, "Bom, Bom, Bom!" The whole spectacle was weird and eerie.

At some point, our children's maid Janine and Claire the cook asked, "Can we go out to the rah-rah?" We answered, "Sure," whereupon Siofra and Embry began jumping up and down, pleading, "Oh, we want to go too, we want to go too!" Since we absolutely didn't feel any personal danger or threat whatsoever, and upon Claire and Janine assuring us that the kids would be quite safe, we let them go to see the rah-rah up close.

In retrospect, I know that it sounds kind of strange to let your two young children attend a Voodoo jubilee in Haiti, but all our fears were allayed by the fact that we knew these people, and we felt safe around them. Then again, to gaze out the window and see all these black Haitians with drums banging, whips cracking, songs booming, voices shouting and incense burning, and to spy the little white faces of our two children in the middle of the crowd, really gave Noreen and me a peculiar feeling. It was quite strange, but quite safe at the same time. We were able to keep the crowd in sight, and the kids were only gone for a short time.

A humorous thing occurred when Noreen's mother once paid us a visit in Haiti. We arranged for her to stay at the glamorous Hotel Oloffson in Port-au-Prince, and we also took a room there. Noreen and I knew that one of the welcoming touches was for freshly-made rum punches to be delivered to guests after checking in, and we were somewhat disappointed when ours were not delivered. Why not? They were ALL mistakenly sent to my mother-in-law's room, and she had done an admirable job of drinking every one.

Speaking of Haitian hotels reminds me of the grand opening of a posh hotel in Port-au-Prince, which Baby Doc himself attended, since the construction was based on his concept of grandeur, including a small pool for each room. Unfortunately, its location was grossly out of place—it was in the poorest section of the city. It was certainly not conducive for hotel customers to stay there.

Moving on to more mundane matters, arranging to receive a telephone line in Haiti was a big production. There were two options: You could either apply and then wait several years for one, or you could find someone who knew someone in the telephone company who knew where the lines were, pay him $400 and acquire your phone hook-up quickly. Since it was vital for me to be in touch with the airport at all times, we decided to do the latter.

In fact, getting hooked up to the main water line and the electrical line meant considering the same two choices that I mentioned above. That was just typical Haiti.

The appropriate word that was used in Haiti to describe such illegal or unusual hookups was a "cumberland." For example, if you wanted water for your house, you had to do a cumberland to the water line; ditto with electricity or telephone service. Apparently, this term was coined after a U.S. Marine named Cumberland who was stationed in Haiti during our occupation in the early 20th century. Evidently, Cumberland was quite adept at mending, fixing and jury-rigging mechanical items, so much so that the locals started calling any sort of contrivance or jury-rig a cumberland.

For example: Years prior to our arrival, Butch Ashton had run a water line from a local reservoir to his home, at great expense. At first, the water pressure was tremendous and there was plenty of water to meet his household needs; however, over the ensuing years, many people cumberlanded onto Butch's water line, and the water pressure had steadily decreased. He estimated that a hundred people along his water line had tapped into it. There was absolutely nothing he could do about the situation except live with it.

Haiti was—and remains today—a complex country to describe or discuss. Physically and geographically, the country provided immense, magnificent panoramas. Its climate was very conducive to agriculture and farming. Its native peoples were friendly, welcoming and helpful. Parties and receptions that we attended always had a mixture of guests from black-black to white-white and every shade in between. Any color or racial problem was non-existent: There was absolutely no racism or differentiation between races and cultures, although the lighter-colored peoples and the whites possessed most of the economic power. Maybe that was balanced out by the fact that the wealthy, darker blacks wielded the political clout in the country.

There's another story that comes to mind which illustrates the typical Haitian senseless thinking.

An interesting hijacking attempt occurred on one of our flights in 1975, shortly before we returned to the States. Frank Etter was the pilot involved—he was an engaging fellow from Switzerland, about 25 years old, who spoke three languages and performed as a jazz musician in his spare time. He had just earned his commercial pilot's license and wanted to build up airtime with us before he applied to one of the major airlines. Somehow, he had also become a friend of Baby Doc; I believe that they enjoyed listening to live music together, perhaps arising from Frank's various jazz gigs.

Anyway, Frank was flying a Haiti Air Dehavilland turboprop Twin Otter from Port-au-Prince to Cap-Haïtien when a local Haitian snuck up on him from behind and placed a machete across his throat, saying in Creole, "I want to go to Cuba." Why anyone would want to go to Cuba, I don't know, but it probably showed how bad life was in Haiti at that moment.

Quick-thinking Frank immediately replied, "We don't have enough fuel to reach Cuba, we'll have to stop and pick up some more." So, he and the co-pilot landed the plane on a small, dusty, dirt road outside the small town of Gonaives, on Haiti's west coast, about 30 miles from their scheduled destination. Then he persuaded the hijacker to let him walk into town to purchase some gasoline. Needless to say, upon Frank's return, he was accompanied by the police, in force, and the culprit was easily taken into custody. The passengers? They were upset because they had to first return to Port-au-Prince, thereby having their travel plans severely disrupted.

When Frank first told me this story, I thought it was a joke, and that he was making it all up. He wasn't. In the final analysis, that probably sounds like a bizarre scenario to most people, but it was just totally believable for Haiti. That poorly conceived hijacking incident confirmed to me that the level of sophistication and worldliness of Haitians was minimal or non-existent. Their innocence was astonishing.

When I later talked to Butch Ashton about this attempted skyjacking, and inquired about the fate of the would-be hijacker, Butch replied, "I think he died of lead poisoning." Ouch.

Frank Etter married a Haitian woman of Lebanese descent and eventually moved to the Middle East. Although I haven't seen him since 1976, I heard that he has been flying as a captain for Saudi Arabian Airlines for some time.

Let me briefly tell another story about Cuba. While getting a routine blood pressure check, I met a Cuban doctor who was practicing on Grand Turk. Originally, we were seen by a group of British doctors, but the locals decided that they didn't want to spend the extra money to access their better medical services, so we ended up with Cubans. The government in Havana rented them out to the Turks and Caicos, but took most of their salaries.

Anyway, the Cuban doctor would always press me for an answer to his plea, "Can you get me into the United States?" He would continue, "I am not here out of loyalty to Fidel." Those medical people just wanted to be able to live freely and receive the benefits of the entire salary that they earned. It certainly made me wonder why anyone would want to go to Cuba voluntarily.

Anyway, by 1973 our little Haitian national airline had officially become Haiti Air Inter. At one point, we explored the idea of the airline becoming an international carrier. Jack put me in touch with some people at Hughes Air West, a West Coast airline that had management contracts to run the airlines in several undeveloped countries— Liberia, Saudi Arabia, Nigeria and other various odd places. The people at Hughes were receptive to Haiti Air Inter becoming an international airline, so I flew to California and back several times to follow up on this idea.

In due course, the Hughes people came down to Haiti where we finally worked out a deal: We could establish a Haitian national flying carrier that would be owned by the Haitians and operated by Turks and Caicos Airways. The aircraft would be leased from the Hughes Corporation, which would also provide some of the necessary management expertise.

We had everything figured out and planned, beginning with a Boeing 727-200, a mid-size, narrow-body, three-engine jet aircraft, on a daily passenger-run schedule to New York City and Miami. Then, the aircraft would have shifted into cargo configuration for a night trip to Miami. The entire projected out-of-pocket cost to the Haitian government was $100,000, which was not an unreasonable amount to start an international airline almost guaranteed to make a profit, due to the large number of Haitian passengers who would be making roundtrips.

That's when the Haitian government became involved, and you can probably figure out what happened. They believed that it was some great trick or ruse by foreigners, and they refused to endorse or approve our business plan, saying that they didn't have $100,000 to spend. Of course, this was ridiculous bunk. Baby Doc had just spent that much money on his eighth and ninth Mercedes, not to mention the half-million dollars on a new yacht—named *Twiggy* after the popular, stick-thin model that he admired back then. Obviously, they possessed sufficient funds; however, there was no way that Haitian government officials would invest in anything that might be long-term, meaning anything over thirty days.

Ultimately, we realized that was just the way the airline business worked in Haiti; but, having done so much planning, we were much discouraged over the unhappy conclusion of events. I wondered if there was any future in it for me whatsoever. Any future at all.

Chapter 12: Farewell, Haiti

"Of course the humans in Haiti have hope. They hope to leave."
—*P.J. O'Rourke*

To make these gloomy matters worse, the Haitian government announced in 1975 that they were going to take over this little internal airline of ours. I guess they were convinced that we were just minting money and carrying it out of the country in planeloads. Basically, they wanted to expel TCA and make me an employee of the government so I could still run the airline. To me, that didn't sound any better than the earlier offer to make me a Colonel in the Haitian Air Force.

Shortly after learning about these Haitian plans, and fearing that the government might attempt to stop or forcibly detain us, I met with the boys one day and told them, "Okay, this is it. Tomorrow morning, we go. Be ready and fueled up." The next morning, we still didn't know for sure what the government was going to do, but there was no way in hell that I was going to make us or our aircraft vulnerable to seizure, so all of us—pilots, mechanics, Noreen and children—just boarded the airplane and left the country. I don't know what happened to our ace mechanic, the Canadian O'Zarko—never saw him again after that. Of course, his wife never liked Haiti and it was difficult for him to please her while they lived there, so who knows.

After we left, the Haitian Air Force took over and attempted to operate the routes and schedules with DC-3s. That plan didn't go very well. Believe it or not, Butch

Ashton eventually phoned me and asked if I could return on a *consultancy* basis for a while, including providing additional planes and restoring the service that we originally established. Maintaining my friendship with Butch and not wanting to burn any bridges, I agreed to assist them. Funny how things work out sometimes.

Immediately going to work for the Haitians I just left, I used my connections in New York and Fort Lauderdale to arrange the purchase of a couple of aircraft. As it turned out, one of the funniest things in this venture was spending several hundred thousand dollars to buy used Britten-Norman Islanders for the Haitians because they didn't want to pay money for the Turboprops—the de Havilland Twin Otters. Both the sellers in New York and Florida assumed that, since I was negotiating on behalf of the Haitian government, I was going to expect at least a 10% kickback on the entire deal. Not having done this sort of transaction before, I guess that I didn't quite get it.

It appeared that no one who heard about this transaction could ever fathom that I would turn down the opportunity for a substantial and lucrative under-the-table commission on the aircraft sales. However, it did leave a very good taste in the Haitians' mouths, and I was always welcome in Haiti for many years after that deal. It's always nice to store up the intangible asset of goodwill that allows you to return to places around the world.

Despite the wondrous beauty of its countryside, Haiti had significant deficits. For one, it was horribly overcrowded. When we resided there, it had become so overpopulated and impoverished that the only source of cooking fuel was timber from the trees. We would fly over the mountains after a heavy rain and observe the topsoil just cascading off the slopes, down the rivers and out to the rolling sea; indeed, for miles out to sea, all around Haiti's coast, one could watch the country's vital topsoil flowing away. The Haitian third of Hispaniola had become so deforested that the precious earth was washed away in every deluge. Of course, erosion like that also affects the quality of farming and harvested crops. No doubt this vicious cycle endures today.

Examining the history of the country, one can see great potential. Believe it or not, in the 1700s, Haiti was the richest colony in the New World and made routine life in the 13 colonies of United States look like subsisting on a so-called poor farm. In fact, the once-common French saying "rich as a creole" directly referred to Haiti, since that country exported hundreds of millions of dollars of goods from its sugar, coffee, cotton, indigo, and cocoa plantations to France.

It's also a little-known fact that John James Audubon, the famous naturalist and painter with many Louisville and Kentucky connections, was born in Haiti in 1785.

Cap-Haïtien, on the country's north coast, was once the richest port city in all the New World. Although the remnants of its grand, beautiful buildings remain, it's become a dirty, run-down community over the years. Historical preservation in the United States is valued much more than in Haiti, where magnificent but decaying architectural structures are more likely to be allowed to deteriorate or even ripped down. Preservationists in the U.S. would have a fit if they saw how Haitians treated these masterpieces. It's a sad and sorry state of affairs.

In addition, there were times when I realized how unpredictable and dangerous the dominant military culture of Haiti could be. Most often, there was absolutely no respect shown to the citizenry of Haiti—or, at times, foreigners—by its army or police force.

An example of that occurred when the Emperor of Ethiopia, either Haile Selassie or his son Amha—I'm not certain which—laid over very briefly in Port-au-Prince to refuel during a lengthy flight. As a casual observer, one of our pilots with a camera started to take photos of this historic occasion. A Haitian Army security guard quickly and loudly chambered a round and, in a menacing manner, pointed his weapon at the head of our pilot, who quickly retreated. That's the way that the armed forces in Haiti acted. You just didn't talk back to or disobey any order from a policeman or soldier who would think nothing of shooting you dead.

On a daily basis, those were the facts of life in Haiti. You had to understand and accept the reality that it was governed by a dictatorship and there were no preconceived notions of fairness and equity.

As I indicated earlier, in 1975 we decided that our airline business was facing serious challenges in Haiti, so we packed up on a moment's notice and flew back to Grand Turk. Poor Noreen had to move out of that grand house in LaBoule and leave behind all the beautiful Voodoo curtains that she had sewn.

When I returned to Haiti for a visit in 1984, it was basically unchanged; even though eight years had passed since I set foot in the country, it still had the same government, politics, infrastructure and unique way of doing business.

Butch Ashton was still involved in 16 different businesses; Tipouche was still the personal secretary to the President; wealthy families still possessed the political power; Baby Doc was still shipping money out of the country to his foreign bank accounts; the ordinary Haitians remained profoundly poor, perhaps even worse off than when I departed in 1976. In addition, other significant issues and controversies had arisen.

Due to the many risks that potential visitors perceived, tourism had considerably decreased, and cruise ships no longer stopped in Port-au-Prince; as a result, many hotel beds went empty. During my visit, I personally paid a call on several hotels where I was acquainted with people, including the popular and glamorous Hotel Oloffson, and they were all mostly vacant. The Hotel Oloffson was featured as the Hotel Trianon in Graham Greene's noted 1966 novel *The Comedians*, which was about political suppression and terrorism under the rule of Papa Doc.

Although Haitians had—and still have—a reputation for being talented artists and fantastic painters, the various art galleries that I visited were empty. When I talked to people I knew in those locales, they just shook their heads and said, "no business."

Foreign dollars were no longer flowing, or even trickling, into the nation. It was very sad; economically, Haiti could be termed a basket case, with a multitude of incurable financial problems.

Why? The answer in one word was AIDS. People were afraid that if they went to Haiti, they would contract AIDS. Folks believed the popular misconception that AIDS started in Haiti. It's entirely possible that the great HIV/AIDS scare of the 1980s may still be preventing tourists from visiting and exploring the country as in the past; although the natural disasters that have occurred in the last few years have also certainly hindered tourism. Perhaps that prejudice regarding AIDS still persists, despite the medical advances that have taken place over the years to treat that horrible disease, and the knowledge about its origins.

Thirty to forty years ago, I was certain that anyone who wanted to overthrow the Haitian government and seize the country could have done so—the Communists, the Cubans or whomever—but who would have wanted to deal with all those long-standing difficulties?

Interestingly, it was a request from a Louisville connection that led me to return to Haiti in 1984. My childhood friend from my Rudy Lane days—J. Paul Keith III, who had become a lawyer—approached me about an issue he was working on. He represented a Kentucky tobacco farm owner who had acquired a tobacco plantation in Haiti. His client's agreements to sell the tobacco were going down the tubes, and Paul asked me to go down there and ask around about the cigarette business and commerce to see if I could obtain more information about what was occurring.

So, I travelled to Haiti and made inquiries. Upon my return, I reported to him that the Dominican Republic farmers were illegally sneaking their cigarettes into the country to compete with the Haitian product. What happened after that, I don't know.

At one time, selling cigarettes was a big deal in Haiti. The poor locals would sell them one-by-one from the side of the road to motorists driving by. North Americans called them sticksales. Noreen was always trying to quit that nicotine habit, but often couldn't resist those sticksales. The most popular brand was Comme Il Faut cigarettes. Coincidentally, Compagnie des Tabacs Comme Il Faut, an international tobacco company based in Port-au-Prince, is owned by Luckett, Inc. of Louisville. It is the only cigarette maker in Haiti, manufacturing both Comme Il Faut and Point brands which are heavily marketed locally.

By the way, the wonderful residence Villarosa came to a sad end on January 12, 2010 when the horrendous 7.0 magnitude earthquake, with its epicenter near Port-au-Prince, struck Haiti. Villarosa was destroyed completely, becoming a pile of rubble.

To end these memories and opinions about Haiti, here is a final word about Tipouche Duyon. Many years after I had left the Islands and Haiti in my rear-view mirror, I was in JFK Airport in New York City when, quite by coincidence, I saw him hurrying along, carrying several bags. "Eh, Tipouche," I hollered, "Koman ou ye?" ("How are you?") He dropped his bags, turned around quickly with a very apprehensive look on his face and then figured out who it was. We spoke briefly, and he departed. It appears that when you are intensely involved in Haitian politics or government, you're always looking over your shoulder, half-scared of what or who will be there.

Part II: My Life after the Islands

Chapter 13: Hello, Virginia

In 1975, when we departed Haiti and returned to Grand Turk, I resumed being general manager of Turks and Caicos Airways for a time. Still disappointed over the failure to establish an international airline carrier in Haiti, I maintained close contact with Jack Real and all the Howard Hughes people with whom I had become friendly—I was still looking for some position a little bigger and better. A couple of times I travelled to California for job interviews, mostly airline management positions, and I hoped that something attractive would become available.

Noreen and I also decided that it would be too difficult to continue raising our children in the Turks and Caicos Islands, for a variety of reasons. In addition, we didn't want to become permanent ex-patriots like so many of the residents were, and we calculated that it would be difficult to save enough money to retire, based on what I was earning at that time.

As we prepared to leave the Islands on which I had spent so much time, I received an unexpected honor—the Turks and Caicos Islands Medal. Engraved "EMBRY RUCKER 1967-1976" on one side, it was presented to me without fanfare or special ceremony. The medal was awarded to recognize my service with distinction in the field of aviation, especially for what I accomplished in the Islands during my ten years flying there.

Finally, something hopeful developed on the job front: Nigeria. Yes, the Hughes people perhaps wanted me to assist with their airlines in Nigeria, Yemen, and other places that sounded horrible to me and that I didn't want to travel to. When all the dust settled, though, my official administrative assignment was going to be in Saudi Arabia, where I would serve as the general manager of the internal Saudi Arabian Airlines—with no piloting involved. This would have been a nice step up the job the airline ladder for me and presented a stimulating managerial position with greater responsibilities and opportunities.

So, in early 1976, the whole family and I moved back to the United States where I began to pursue licensing as an air frame and power plant mechanic, a license that the Hughes people wanted me to have. For a few weeks, I went to a cram school down in Nashville, Tennessee. As far as engine and aircraft mechanics were concerned, I'd had all the practical experience necessary, but I needed the formal schooling in order to learn the official rules, regulations and protocols. In any event, I went to school, took the tests, passed them with flying colors and became officially licensed as an air frame and power plant mechanic.

While all my Tennessee educational efforts were taking place, Noreen and I had begun to establish our own home base by purchasing a farm in Virginia, not too far away—about 70 miles—from Dulles International Airport in Washington. Our place covered than a hundred acres and included an old house, part log-built and part clapboard, which dated back to 1780. The structure had been improved in the 1800s with a slate roof. It was in a scenic, sleepy part of Virginia called Kent Store, not too far from Ruckersville, the Virginia town settled by my ancestors long ago. In my mind, I conjured up fantasies and visions that the land had belonged to my forefathers in the 1600s; unfortunately, this scenario went unproven.

Gearing up for my soon-to-be Saudi Arabian adventure, we even purchased clothes that would be suitable for the Middle East climate. Noreen and I worked on housing, budgets and expenses for living in Riyadh, the capital and largest city of Saudi Arabia, which would be our Middle Eastern home base.

Then, quite suddenly, while waiting for my appointment to be finally approved, all our plans came crashing down—Howard Hughes died in Mexico on April 5, 1976. He had moved there from the Bahamas, where he had spent the previous three years. His passing generated significant turmoil and upheaval within all the companies of the Hughes business empire. There were major reversals of fortune: Some folks who had great influence were abruptly out, and other people who didn't possess influence were unexpectedly in. Suffice it to say that much confusion reigned. For a really well-documented account of this period in the Hughes Corporation, I suggest that you refer to the book *The Asylum of Howard Hughes*, by Jack G. Real (with Bill Yenne), published in 2003 by Xlibris Corporation. It provides fascinating reading.

Well, in the middle of all this transition mess, I suspected that my friend Jack was dreadfully busy, along with the others in California who originally tabbed me for Saudi Arabia; as a result, someone else ended up slipping into the job that I expected to fill. So there I was, all dressed up with no place to go. Plus, I now had a sizeable property investment in my Virginia farm. Unemployment was only one of a multitude of problems that I faced. The course and direction of my professional and personal lives had changed without a bit of warning, due to the death of a person whom I had never met.

Chapter 14: Chicken and Grits

One of the many things stressing me out that I faced during this period of unemployment and upheaval was living with my parents. Although they were very supportive of our plans, I thought that they might be drained from having the four of us live with them—Siofra and Embry were 7 and 4 at the time—and I certainly didn't wish to intrude on my parents any longer than was necessary. We placed our newly-acquired farm on the market for sale, but no buyers showed any interest; as a matter of fact, it took a couple of years to sell it. We had never moved onto the property or resided there. That was very frustrating.

However, my luck changed for the better when I discovered a Help Wanted ad in the *Washington Post*. Showell Farms, Inc., a large chicken operation in Maryland's Eastern Shore area was seeking a pilot. My prospective corporate employer raised and slaughtered chickens, then distributed them to markets and processing plants. Showell was a solid, old-line firm, founded in 1908.

Oddly enough, during my initial interview for this position as the company's corporate pilot, I learned that the fellow meeting with me formerly worked for one of the Hughes organizations, so we spent much time discussing mutual acquaintances. Finally, he observed, "You know, you seem like you got a lot more on the ball that being just a corporate pilot, and we need a corporate fleet director. The salary is better, and I believe that you can do the job. Are you interested?" Well, I had no idea what a corporate fleet director was, but I suspected that I'd oversee all the trucks and vehicles for the corporation. So, I accepted their offer, and, sure enough, I became responsible for the organization and operation of about 200 vehicles located in Maryland, North Carolina and the Florida panhandle.

My new position meant that we had to take the children out of school again, since we decided it was more convenient to move closer to my primary worksite. We settled into a townhouse condominium that we rented; it was situated on a golf course near Ocean City Maryland in a town called, of all things, Berlin. Noreen, showing her typical fortitude and grit, was again at my side every step of the way, from strange place to strange place, without complaint. This was an especially difficult move because, in that part of the country, we did not know one other person; in fact, this was a summer resort area, and we were the only permanent residents. But we didn't stay there long.

It didn't take me long to ascertain that my new company was functioning in complete chaos and utter confusion. Although I was employed and getting paid, I spent a lot of time trying to figure out what in the hell it was all about. The corporate owner, Mr. Alan Guerreri, one of the family that founded the company, was absolutely brutal to his employees; at the weekly executive staff meetings, all the division managers were so cowed that they told him exactly what he wanted to hear, despite the truth of the matter. There was just disorder and turmoil all over the place—how the company made money, I have no idea, even though it was the tenth largest poultry firm in the United States.

They did have a sophisticated computer program that was designed to keep track of all the chickens, baby chicks, eggs, chicken feed, vehicles and every other damned thing they owned. However, it was hopelessly inaccurate. Incredibly detailed computer printouts would be sent to me showing that we maintained 50 more vehicles than I knew actually existed within the company; and, the following week, it would show 30 *less* trucks. On one occasion, one of these printouts indicated that the same truck had just had four engines and 17 mufflers replaced! There was just no way of obtaining and verifying the correct underlying information. Not a good situation for the new corporate fleet director.

When I mentioned this dilemma to the owner—my new boss—at one of the staff meetings, he just exploded! Watching him scream, shout, curse and foam at the mouth, I finally decided that this unexpected response was nonsense—I didn't need this outlandish, bizarre conduct. So, from then on, I just kept my mouth closed. If he didn't want to hear what was really happening within his own company, I wasn't going to be the sap who told him.

After several months with the company, I witnessed something memorable on a trip down South. A group of us were travelling to Florida to inspect our newest operation down there; our party included the heads of the grain operation and the live haul operation and several other division chiefs. A brand-new employee also accompanied us—he was a young nutritionist from New York City, right out of college, who was hot stuff on the subject of chicken nutrition.

During the morning of the trip, our company plane needed to stop in Georgia to refuel. While waiting, we decided to eat breakfast at the local short-order restaurant. Most of us being Southerners, we ordered grits, eggs and ham. Our greenhorn nutritionist from New York ordered bacon and scrambled eggs, whereupon the waitress asked, "You want any grits?" He replied, "What's grits?" She put her hands on her hips, reared back and bellowed, "Well, grits is grits, you dumb ass!" The rest of us just cracked up and fell on the floor laughing.

Anyway, my co-workers were a pleasant group, but what a screwed-up corporate enterprise to work for. Eventually in 1995, Perdue Farms bought out Showell, creating the nation's third-largest poultry producer. But I was long gone by then.

Chapter 15: Champion Saves the Day

It was around this time in early 1977 that my father called me with some news about Champion Wood Products, the Jeffersonville, Indiana company that he had founded and managed. My life's direction was about to change once again.

My father had been teaching Business Management at nights at the University of Louisville when he developed a sideline business called the Rucker Corporation, in the late 1940's. He made cheap coffee tables, end tables and similar small furnishings and sold them through the Reinisch Brothers distributing company in Chicago. You may recall that I previously mentioned his work and fascination with plywood.

After Pop's business went bankrupt around 1952, he bounced back with Champion. His business plan involved acquiring wood scraps, which he then cut into smaller parts for resale to the wooden cabinet industry for use as shelf backs or corner braces, for example. He achieved some early success in this venture. So, in 1956, he incorporated for a total capital investment of $600 and hired a salaried employee, Joe Byron, to oversee the business when Pop relocated to Virginia. After Joe died, his son Steve took over for him.

Beginning in 1974, my father had been talking to me about assuming the reins of the business—at that time, he was in Virginia undergoing heart bypass surgery, and I was involved in the Haitian airline startup. Then, a few years later, after he had run for the Virginia state legislature and lost, Pop informed me that the manager of the wood operation, Steve Byron, appeared to be having some trouble overseeing the company. He then asked if I would be interested in returning to the Southern Indiana area to take over the business. In his usual way, Pop made it sound just wonderful. In truth, his kind offer came at the perfect time for me. Note that this was not a venture in which Rudy was at all interested.

After working for the chaotic, goofy chicken producer, I was looking forward to a change of pace. Going back to the old hometown area sounded fantastic, as did a larger salary and a company car. My assumption was that the business was making money, just as it always had done, although Pop declined to tell me anything specific about the company's finances. So, I decided to give it a shot, and Noreen called the movers again.

Upon our return, I started stumbling around Champion trying to determine exactly what was taking place. The company's official address was: Champion Wood Products, Inc., One Champion Road, P.O. Box 178, Jeffersonville, Indiana 47131. It was located just behind the Jeffersonville Quartermaster Depot, better known as The Quadrangle, which originally opened in 1874 as a military warehouse. Our specific worksite was first built for use as a saddle and harness repair shop during the Spanish-American War of 1898.

When I arrived to take over Champion, Pop was facing a few problems. For one, his former company manager had gone into business for himself and was trying to steal all of Champion's customers. Now, Pop had a plant manager named Mike Gladish who had worked there for a while. Wanting to get him more actively involved and committed to the business, I sold him a share in the company. Although he had become a partner, Gladish only had a 20% interest in the company, so I was still able to call the shots. It worked.

At first, I thought that maybe I was just stupid, but then I discovered that nobody else there seemed to really know what kind of standard business practices were being used either. After the prior manager left, there was no one in charge. Several months later, Liberty National Bank let us know that it was getting antsy, asking where our accounting statements were, whether we were making a profit and just what the heck was going on at Champion.

Finally, weary from plugging all the leaks in the business, Pop and I sat down one day and listed all our assets and liabilities; unfortunately, our computation showed that Champion had a negative net worth—we were literally bankrupt. So, we agreed to just throw that piece of paper away—we certainly don't want the bank or anyone else to know that the company was in that bad shape. Although we knew we could make the business profitable again because we still retained both loyal customers and a workable system, Liberty—the bank we were dealing with at the time—was getting very impatient, implying that we didn't know what we were doing. And they were very nearly correct, because we were only generating accounting statements once a year, which we thought was acceptable at the time.

It occurred to me that I had a friend, Grier Martin, who worked at First National Bank as the Vice President in the Small Business division. So, I called Grier and explained, "We have a good operation, but we just don't know what's going on right now. We can and will make money, but we need a loan to pay off our other existing loans at the other bank and to provide us with some operating capital." Grier's positive response to our plea was exceptional; he really went out on a limb for us. First National agreed to loan us the money we requested, with one of the conditions being that we retain an accounting company to prepare proper monthly statements and other necessary financials.

As a result, we had a visit that I will never forget with Armand Ostroff and David Livsey, principals from the accounting firm of Deming, Malone, Livsey and Ostroff, which was then just in its inception. Referred to us by Grier Martin, these two gentlemen came over to Jeffersonville, briefly inspected our reports and records and agreed to provide us with the proper accounting services. To begin, they stated that the initial fee would be $800 for the first segment of work. We said, "Fine, go ahead." In response, they said firmly, "In advance!" It was precisely at that point, with that answer, that I truly realized the gravity of our perilous financial situation. On a side note, I joked with them for the next 30 years about this comment—it appears that they needed the money just as much as we did.

As it turned out, Deming Malone was a great help to us. They assigned a young fellow named Dick Sipes from Breckenridge County to handle our account; he was very helpful and assisted us in straightening out all of Champion's financial woes. From his advice and consultation, we realized that we employed too many people, had no cost controls and were making way too many quality and quantity mistakes when we purchased lumber. With Dick's assistance, we turned things around and actually made a profit, although our cash flow was still very tight.

Then, in August of 1979, we were in good enough fiscal shape to acquire another company. Paying cash, we bought Sylvan Products of Shepherdsville, then owned by Lee Duvall. Sylvan made interior wooden frames for upholstered furniture, and their dozen employees moved over to Champion. In retrospect, that period was the proverbial calm before the storm.

In charge for less than two years, I had been doing everything I could to make Champion an attractive workplace for our employees: providing health insurance, establishing a profit-sharing plan and giving bonuses and incentives. One successful program that I started was to establish a target amount for the week's production; after reaching that goal, the employees could go home for the remainder of the week. I was sympathetic to the working conditions of the workers.

However, one of our employees was working on behalf of Teamsters Local 89 to unionize, and a vote was eventually scheduled to be taken. The main organizer was a violent fellow who one day punched me in the face, broke my nose, knocked me unconscious and was kicking me as I came to. Ultimately, we won by a few votes, and there was no union.

Shortly after that, I faced a major crisis with the company. Champion was hit by a devastating fire in October of 1979—probably arson, but we never learned for sure who started it or was involved. The headline for the article in the *Courier-Journal* on October 23 read, "Wind-driven fire destroys Jeffersonville warehouse." Although the ruined building was the smallest of the seven structures that Champion owned at that site, it housed about one-third of our finished inventory; the total amount of the loss was about $125,000. We were very lucky that it was that warehouse and not the plant that was destroyed. It was the first fire that Champion had in its 27 years of existence.

The cause of the fire was never determined. Who did it? Well, the Teamsters were upset with me at the time. The Fire Marshall interviewed *me*, probably thinking that I may have been involved, but nothing could have been further from the truth. My opinion is that the fire was set by someone angry about our differences over the unionization of the company. To make matters worse, our insurance carrier initially did not agree to reimburse us for our losses.

In the early 1980s, after we got back on our feet from the fire, the business faced severe financial stress, and I almost sold it to noted Louisville businessman Jim Patterson, owner of Pattco LLC and founder of Rally's and Long John Silver's restaurants. Our accountant told us that

Patterson owned a company in Bowling Green that made wooden directors chairs—and that he may be interested in buying out Champion. It turned out that he was.

However, after six months, the negotiations and deal with Patterson fell through; but, we still survived without taking bankruptcy. My attorney and friend—J. Paul Keith—wrote a letter to our creditors telling them of our survival plan, in which they would receive an estimated 85 to 90% payback on their money. There were no objections to this; ultimately, the creditors received 92% of their money back immediately, with the rest paid back over time. We auctioned off some machinery, leased part of the building, cut payroll, and settled with the insurer for our fire losses by taking an offer from them rather than filing a lawsuit. It all worked out. My credit was still golden.

Overall, despite these setbacks, I was pleased with the job that I did at Champion. After putting my savings into the company, taking out loans and avoiding bankruptcy, I was able to turn Champion Wood Products around and make it profitable. It was still going well when I started thinking about offering it for sale in the mid-1990s, and I eventually did sell in 1998.

The actual sale of Champion was quite a process. I had a potential buyer who was somewhat leery of taking it on, so I brought him on board and he worked for me for about six months, learning the business from the inside. He enjoyed it, and we made a deal after that trial period. The buyers were Andy Thurstone and my partner Mike Gladish. They wanted to buy it on a 50-50 split, but I insisted that one partner have authority to make decisions, so Mike ended up with 49% and Andy 51%. The company is still operating in Sellersburg, Indiana, and it employs 88 workers.

Chapter 16: The Rest of My Story

"There is no real ending. It's just the place where you stop the story." —Frank Herbert

After leaving the British West Indies, it was my good fortune to continue leading a life with a variety of challenges and adventures. Allow me to bring you up to date from the 1970s, sometimes in no particular order.

§

Noreen and I certainly faced challenges with the relocation to Louisville when I became involved with the management of Champion. For the kids, it meant transferring to the third school system in less than a year. Plus, we returned to Louisville in January 1978, at the start of one of the coldest winters in its history—even the Ohio River froze over, for only the fourth time in the last 160 years. The winter weather conditions were just miserable.

At first, we moved into an apartment on the ninth or tenth floor in the 800 Building at Fourth and York Streets. At the time it opened in 1963, The 800, as it was called, at 29 stories, was the tallest building in Kentucky, Indiana and Tennessee. Although age and maintenance issues have dimmed its luster over the years until a very recent makeover, the 800 Building was quite the upscale place to reside in that era. Our only vehicle at the time was a 16-year-old pickup truck, and I guarantee you that was the only pickup driven by anyone who resided in that building. Pickups were definitely not cool then, especially at The 800.

In any event, Noreen and I promptly began looking around and in a few months purchased an old house at 7117 Covered Bridge Road in Prospect. It was an old two-story house with plenty of features: an acre lot with trees, horse pasture and small stable, four bedrooms, a wood-burning fireplace in the master bedroom, updated kitchen and 1½ bathrooms, 2-car garage and a smoke house. We only lived there for a year or so before buying a nearby historic house that was near the Prospect Christian Church. It only took a couple of months to sell our home at 7117.

Located at 7123 Covered Bridge Road, the historic James Clore House was built around 1847 and had been owned and occupied by Clore descendants until we bought it in 1978.

The house was situated about a half-mile off Covered Bridge Road on a long gravel roadway. The entire property comprised 40 acres, and we split the purchase with two other buyers. We ended up with 20 acres and the old house and barn. Surrounded by trees, it was a wonderful, scenic location, right in Prospect.

The realtor who assisted us in buying that property was Mike Skelton, and that deal began a long-time professional relationship with him. We have retained him to assist us in at least 10 real estate transactions. Coincidentally, Mike now lives on Rudy Lane, next door to the house where I lived as a boy.

Renovating that home on Covered Bridge Road was no easy task. The front of the house was literally falling off when we bought it. To save it, Noreen and I engaged in some back-breaking work to install 20-foot-long threaded bolts along the front—sort of a homemade idea of mine that worked perfectly. To cut our property taxes, Noreen and I donated a conservation easement on the property to the county.

§

Over the years, I developed a strong interest in hunting and fishing. Although I hadn't hunted that much as a kid, except with a BB gun, I began hunting ducks and geese in the 1980s. Then I got it in my mind to seek bigger game. To that end, I have taken eight trips to Africa to participate in a total of 10 hunting safaris—nine in Zimbabwe and one in Zambia.

In 1988, starting right at the top of the chain, I signed up for a plains-game hunt in Zimbabwe. The locale was a million-acre cattle ranch owned by the English global company Unilever, and the professional hunter who guided me was Butch Walker. Eventually, I would go on two safaris with Butch and at least six with Russell Tarr, who had worked for Butch. Butch and I became fast friends. In fact, he just visited Joanie and me in Louisville for three nights in June 2016; this, during one of his tours of England, Alaska, and the lower 48.

On that first trip, although we were looking for non-dangerous species, I did manage to shoot a leopard. At nighttime! Butch had armed himself with a shotgun, and his instructions to me were, "Don't shoot me, and don't shoot the trackers." These men were carrying an antiquated lighting system involving a battery and a flashlight. When turned on, a reddish light appeared which didn't bother or frighten away the animals.

When we sighted him, the leopard was about 30 yards away in a tree with the bait that had been placed there. My first and only shot hit him between the eyes, and so I became a big-game hunter. Quite an achievement for someone who, up until then, had only pursued birds, ducks and geese.

After bagging kudu, wildebeest, impala, eland and warthog, I came home thinking that would be my one and only trip. But I returned to Africa many times, including my first elephant hunt and kill in the Zambezi Valley in 1990. The locals, by the way, made use of virtually all of that elephant carcass; upon returning 24 hours later to inspect it, the only thing I found was the skull.

Many exciting events occurred on these treks, including an encounter with one of the world's most dangerous poisonous snakes. The puff adder is an aggressive, venomous viper that is found throughout Africa, and is responsible for the most snakebite fatalities on the continent. All I can say is that when I *stepped on* the puff adder, it must have been sleeping, and that's why I am still here to record these stories.

Then there was one of the times we hunted the cape buffalo, which is highly dangerous to humans due to its unpredictable nature and size—up to 2,000 pounds. Being a member of the group of extremely dangerous animals called the Big Five, it is highly sought after by big game hunters; lions and humans are basically its only predators.

There were five of us out that day looking for the buffalo: Russell Tarr, who was our professional hunter, the two trackers, Noreen and me. We found a buffalo—I shot and hit it, but didn't kill it. Off it went, running away. After following its trail for a while, we found it—or it found us. In any event, it unexpectedly charged out of some brush, but my second shot hit it directly in the brain. Its charge was stopped by my bullet, and the buffalo's carcass wound up exactly four paces away from where I was standing.

When I turned around, I found Noreen safely up a tree—the trackers, too! In the excitement of the buffalo's deadly charge, one of the trackers had pushed Noreen aside and thrown his machete down so he could use both hands and climb faster. The machete had struck her in the knee and sliced it open badly. Our hunter was furious, and he yelled at the trackers, "You are bad people, you are bad people!" At least it gave Noreen a good story to tell, because she had a scar there for the rest of her life. "See what happens when you go hunting with Embry," she would say to friends.

It is so important to have a good professional in charge when you are on a hunting safari. In Africa, such pros are labeled professional hunters, and are required to undergo a rigorous training program of study to become qualified and licensed. In the United States, such people are referred to as guides, and may or may not be as skilled and trained.

Since the buffalo incident above, I have hunted with Russell at least six times. He is the consummate professional, and he has many stories of his time serving with the Rhodesian Light Infantry, one of the world's foremost anti-terrorist commando forces until it disbanded in 1980. Russell had the privilege of serving under his father, the Colonel Commanding. Russell was born in Zambia and has both Zimbabwean and South African citizenship. At one point, I presented Russell with a Kentucky Colonel commission that I had nominated him for, and I told him that he was now of equal rank with his father.

In 2008, on another hunting safari with professional hunter Martin Pieters, we sought the hippopotamus, one of the largest living land mammals. These semiaquatic animals are very aggressive towards humans, whom they will attack whether in boats or on land, sometimes with no apparent provocation; they are widely considered to be one of the most dangerous large animals in Africa.

Early on, I advised Martin that I wanted to take a hippo—but on land, not in the water. So, we proceeded to a small bay off Lake Kariba, the world's largest man-made lake and reservoir by volume, situated along the border between Zambia and Zimbabwe. Happening upon a grounded hippo that appeared to have been severely wounded in a fight with another hippo, I prepared to put it out of its misery—when suddenly it lumbered back into the knee-deep water.

Thinking it may be on a sand bar, I shot it; however, it keeled over and sank under the water out of sight. Martin then told Dalton Tink, the apprentice hunter who was following him, to jump in and attach a rope to the hippo. Obediently, young hunter Tink, aware of the many crocodiles that we had seen in the area, literally put a knife between his teeth and dove into the water.

Reappearing after being under the surface for a while, Tink reported that the animal was in a depression in the bay's floor; Martin gave him a rope and told him to get it done. On one gulp of air, Tink dove, cut a place in the hippo's hide, secured the rope and came up again. Then Martin attached the end of the rope to our Land Rover and pulled the carcass out of the water. After taking what we wanted from the animal, the locals removed its hide and recycled virtually everything else.

When I attended a safari convention in Las Vegas in February 2017, I happened to run into Dalton Tink, and we laughed about that incident. He is one of the newest licensed professional hunters working for Martin Pieters Safaris, and has been described as still having a pit bull mindset. I thanked him for the memories that hippo incident gave me—always funny. Tink replied, "Believe me, I haven't done it again."

Hanging on one of the walls at home is a photo of me with a large, dangerous crocodile—almost two and a half times my size—that I shot in the Ume River in northern Zimbabwe. It was 15 feet long.

Of the Big Five, I have bagged elephant, lion, cape buffalo and leopard—all except the black rhino, a critically endangered species that is rarely hunted legally. My last trip to the Dark Continent was in September 2011, when I shot a sable antelope and a Lichtenstein's hartebeest.

§

Another unique experience I had was hunting quail and nilgai on the King Ranch in the 1980s. This huge spread, located in South Texas between Corpus Christi and Brownsville and near Kingsville, is the largest ranch in Texas, comprising 825,000 acres. Years ago, King Ranch began offering a limited number of low-fence, fair-chase hunts as part of their ongoing wildlife management program.

Upon my arrival, one of the guides was showing me around the property so I could take some test shots with my rifle, when we happened upon a herd of nilgai, or blue cow. This animal is a large Asian antelope that was first introduced to Texas, probably by travelling circuses, some 90 years ago.

My guide remarked that there was a really large bull in the herd, and I ended up taking that bull down. Eventually, the ranch staff took the skull and horns to a professional measurer, who determined that it was the 4th largest nilgai bull ever taken. It's still in the top ten today.

Altogether, I have shot 50 species, and maybe 49 are still listed in records books today, although some may not be so high up. The oribi, a small, slender African antelope, which I shot, was the 11th largest ever taken.

§

In 1984, Noreen and I had an interesting—and vital—connection to a famous Grant's zebra nicknamed "E.Q." It was foaled by our 26-year-old quarter horse Kelly in Shelby County. The birth represented the first successful embryo transfer from an exotic to domestic equine, and it was the first known instance of a horse giving birth to a full-blooded zebra, according to Louisville Zoo officials. The procedure was performed in cooperation with the Louisville Zoo and Equine Services in Simpsonville. Zoo veterinarian William R. Foster, DVM and Equine Specialist Scott D. Bennett, DVM transferred the zebra embryo. Named Equuleus after a constellation of stars, the male zebra was more often referred to as E.Q.

While all births are cause for celebration, this zebra birth was then seen as an important step toward preserving endangered species. The ordinary Grant's zebra was not considered endangered, but zoo officials cited Grevy's and Chapman's zebras as breeds that might be helped. Noreen and I also hoped that such procedures could help augment the rare zebras of the world.

How did all this come about?

Well, we knew Dr. Scott Bennett well from treating the horses that we owned. He called us one afternoon to say that he had just placed four zebra embryos in horses and that he had one left over; he wanted to know if Kelly was in season. Noreen didn't know, and she invited him over to check. When the vet determined that the time was right for our horse, he implanted the embryo. Hers was the only one that took.

About a year later—one month past the usual 11 months for horses—a large group of vets, reporters and farm hands turned out for the birth. We were there with Siofra and Embry. During the birth, I rubbed Kelly's nose and whispered in her ear, although I don't know if that helped Kelly at all. Noreen was interviewed for the big story that appeared in the *Courier-Journal* the next day.

Although we didn't want any publicity about this birth, the unique circumstances of the story caused it to be picked up by wire services and published in countless newspapers. In fact, we received messages and postcards from our friends all over the world. In talking to people, one common misconception was that the foal was half-horse and half-zebra. Not so.

Still hanging in my basement after many years is the Louisville Zoo poster featuring the young zebra. E.Q. left the Louisville Zoo in 1985, but made two brief return visits in 1985 and 1989. He died at the Houston Zoo in 1999.

§

Riding since she was a youngster, Noreen was the horsey-kid in her family in Ireland. In Irish society, everyone joined in to support those who enjoyed riding horses, and her family was no different.

After leaving the Turks and Caicos and moving back to Kentucky, Noreen became interested in becoming a farrier—an equine blacksmith who trims and shoes horses' hooves. She enrolled in a farrier school that operated in Mt. Eden, a small community in Spencer County. Being the only woman in the program, and the only Irish lass, she had quite an experience meeting the other farrier candidates. Eventually she graduated and started to work not only on ours, but on other clients' horses—for a fee, of course.

We never boarded out our horses; in fact, we boarded other owners' horses on our farm. Noreen was a member of the Long Run Hounds, the second oldest hunt club in Kentucky. She was assistant commissioner in Oldham County's Covered Bridge Pony Club in which daughter Siofra was active. Pony Club is the largest equestrian educational program in the world, with many local chapters. Begun in 1972, the Covered Bridge chapter is among the largest and most energetic of the 600 such clubs in the country.

§

Speaking of animals, Embry Rucker finished in the money at the racetrack a few times from 1988 to 1991—Embry Rucker the horse, that is. This colt was owned by my friend Bill Luskey and his brother who were active in horse breeding and training at that time.

A bunch of us were having dinner one day and the talk turned to the naming of colts. Bill explained the rules and regulations and used the name "Embry Rucker" as an example. Well, it turned out that name was not taken, so he actually named a colt after me. It ran all over the thoroughbred circuit, including Aqueduct, Sportsman's Park, Monmouth Park, the Meadowlands, Ellis Park and Fairmount Park, winning at least once.

§

During Christmas of 1989, Noreen and the children and I took a fascinating and action-packed sightseeing trip to Egypt, with free TWA tickets—New York to Paris to Cairo—courtesy of my flight miles. In addition, we were all upgraded to first class because there was extra room up front, and we had free lodging upon our arrival, courtesy of my friend Gray Henry, spiritualist and publisher. While staying in her house in Cairo, we took part in the usual tourist activities such as visiting the Pyramids and the Sphinx, but we also travelled out to the Sinai Peninsula to visit Mount Sinai, the site where God presented Moses with the Ten Commandments.

On our bus trip to Sinai, while travelling through the area where the Six-Day War occurred in 1967 between the Arabs and Israelis, we viewed the grim remains of many wrecked tanks and trucks. In addition, our bus driver made the trip exciting by watching a soap opera on his portable television set while he was driving, occasionally veering off the road.

Upon arrival, we toured Saint Catherine's Monastery, an historic Greek—or Eastern—Orthodox holy place that is supposed to be built over the site where Moses saw the burning bush, as told in the Bible. The monastery also contained a treasure trove of icons and ancient manuscripts. While there, I encountered a monk who spoke English—and who surprisingly identified himself as a native of Salt Lake City, Utah. Not only that, but after further conversation, I discovered that he was a high school classmate of my good friend and Kenyon College classmate from Salt Lake City, Zeese Papanikolas. Small world, indeed. Zeese, 74, is a well-regarded creative writer who has published many books; he now resides in California.

During that trip, we spent Christmas Day on Mt. Sinai. Another memorable incident occurred when young Embry (16), urged on by a camel-driver, suggested that he was willing to trade Siofra (18) to the man in return for a camel. That proposed bargain is occasionally brought up in family discussions even today.

While on that trip, I had the unique pleasure of duck-hunting with a retired Egyptian Army Colonel who had been wounded during the Six-Day War. In anticipation, I had even packed and brought my waders to Cairo. The two of us ventured out to a site along the Nile River in an SUV, accompanied by two Saudis. We set our decoys out and waited for the ducks—mallards and teals—to appear. They did, and we brought down a few. It sounds strange to say this, but in the absence of dogs, two young boys were the retrievers.

After they brought the ducks back, the young Egyptians made a great show of slitting the ducks' throats in front of us—in order to comply with religious requirements for eating them—although I suspect that the animals were already dead from the shot. I brought several back to our housekeeper and explained to her that they were acceptable to eat. Although our two comrades didn't speak much English, we all still had an excellent time on this brief hunting trip in Egypt.

§

Over the years, both of my children became college graduates in far faster time than me. After graduating in 1988 from Louisville Collegiate School, Siofra earned her degree from St. John's College, a private liberal arts college, attending both the Annapolis, Maryland and Santa Fe, New Mexico campuses.

In 1991, Embry III graduated from St. Francis High School in downtown Louisville; it was the ideal place for adolescent Embry to attend. Later, upon entering college and comparing himself to some of the other students, he told me, "Dad, I must have gotten a better education than I thought." After two years at the University of Wyoming in Laramie, he moved to Missoula and graduated from the University of Montana. Embry's wife Leslie is from Palo Alto, California; they live in Encinitas, a beach city in San Diego County.

As I noted before, I am proud of our children. Embry III has become an outstanding professional photographer, and he has many years of experience commercially shooting high-profile clients—including some of the biggest brands in the world—such as Nike, Harley Davidson, North Face, Target, Volvo, Reebok and many, many more. For more about him, you can check out his website at embryrucker. com.

As I write this, Siofra lives on Maryland Avenue in Louisville, just a few blocks away from our house on Glenmary. She has worked in the area of development for private non-profit corporations, including Yew Dell Gardens. She is currently director of advancement for St. Francis School, and I am very proud of her successes.

§

When young Embry was enrolled at Wyoming in the early 1990s, Noreen and I bought 1,000 acres in Wyoming and, with his help, built a nice cabin on that spread. Located out in the country, about 45 minutes from Laramie, it was mainly used by me for hunting, and by son Embry as a place to escape from the rigors of his college studies.

The first time I ever visited that area was as a guest of one of my lumber suppliers at Champion; at that time, we hunted mule deer and antelope. It didn't take long for me to fall in love with hunting in the wide-open spaces of big sky country. Engaging a realtor named Dave Berry, I discovered that he was the owner of a large ranch and was selling parcels of his acreage, so I bought some of his land. The house was nice, nothing special, and we installed a solar electric system and a refrigerator that operated on propane.

However, Noreen was not crazy about it—it was a long trek to Laramie to buy anything, and the elevation of our property was high—about 8,000 feet. So, we put it up for sale after five years, asking a low enough price that we thought it would sell quickly; but, it didn't. So, I did something weird that worked: I raised the price. Then, I had no trouble selling it. With the low price, potential buyers must have thought there was something wrong with it; the higher price made it appear more exclusive. Such is life.

§

Noreen and I also flew to New Zealand, where we spent three superb weeks—though I only hunted for five days. When I attended a safari hunters convention in

Nevada in 1992 or so, I made friends with Dr. Reinald von Meurers, a medical doctor, big-game hunter and author. In a complicated transaction, I basically traded him a hunting trip to British Columbia, and he gave me a trip to New Zealand.

New Zealand is home to some very wily deer, evidenced by my inability to bag even one of them. But that was OK, because the scenery in that country was quite stunning, day in and day out. In fact, Noreen and I agreed that if we were 20 years younger, we would have stayed there. Although I have a niece in Australia, we weren't able to travel there.

§

In 1996, Noreen accompanied me on a hunting trip to Alaska where I was hunting Dall's Sheep, a subspecies of Thinhorn Sheep, found in the subarctic mountain ranges there. It was exhausting climbing the mountains, and we were also on horseback for much of the time. While there, we met and became friendly with Charles J. "Charlie" Fritz, a renowned Western landscape artist who was hunting grizzly bear.

Charlie is an artist with a particular interest and specialty in illustrating the journals of Lewis and Clark. He explained to us how his 100 paintings of the Lewis and Clark expedition of 1804-1806 were purchased by a buyer and then exhibited the first time by Bass Pro Shops, giving him much exposure. He later published a book titled *Charles Fritz: 100 Paintings Illustrating the Journals of Lewis and Clark*.

Since we met, I have maintained contact with Charlie and made some purchases from him, including a painting titled, "Pronghorns on the New Mexico Borderlands," showing some antelope that I hunted.

§

Including both hunting trips and sightseeing destinations, I have travelled to at least 36 foreign countries, in addition to the Turks and Caicos. They are:

Mexico, Belize, Guatemala, Jamaica, Bahamas, Haiti, Dominican Republic, Bermuda, England, Ireland, Scotland, Wales, Andorra, Spain, Switzerland, Monaco, Holland, France, Germany, Italy, Belgium, Austria, Lichtenstein, Luxembourg, Canada, Mexico, Uruguay, Argentina, Micronesia, New Zealand, Zimbabwe, Zambia, Egypt, South Africa and a stopover in Botswana. Plus, the only states that I have *not* set foot in are Louisiana and Vermont.

§

Back to the Islands: In 1998, Noreen and I purchased 2.5 acres of land on Salt Cay from a Malaysian gentleman. Salt Cay is located about eight miles south of Grand Turk. At the time, only about 50 people lived there, and there were no retail or grocery stores whatsoever. Years later, we sold that land to a Californian.

We also bought a run-down, dilapidated cottage on Grand Turk and rehabbed it. The local termites had decimated all the wood, so the house had to be gutted. Generally, the older buildings there were built with yellow pine and a lot of pitch in order to deter termite infestations. Our cottage ended up with a high-pitched roof and plenty of pressure-treated lumber.

Noreen and I would spend two or three months a year at Grand Turk, just enjoying life. Basically, it became our primary residence. Brother Rudy joined us in 2001 and 2006 to relax and go diving with us. Our kids would also join us with our grandchildren—Embry and Siofra always retained good feelings about the Islands. In fact, my son became greatly irritated once when the local customs official stamped his passport as a visitor. He quickly proclaimed to them, "I bearn here!" Much surprised and properly chastened, they redid his paperwork.

As for me, after I had lived in the Islands for several years, I was granted "PRC #4"—meaning that I was the 4th foreigner to be given a Permanent Resident Card. Similar to what we know as a green card, permanent residency refers to a person's visa status; a permanent resident can reside indefinitely within a country of which he or she is not a citizen.

Many years later, after Noreen and I moved back to Grand Turk, I was accorded Belonger status because I had been associated for so many years with the Islands. Belonger status is a legal classification associated with British Overseas Territories. A Belonger is an individual who is free from immigration restrictions regarding the amount of time they may remain in the Turks and Caicos. One way to acquire that status is to be granted a Certificate of Belonger Status by the Governor for having made a significant social or economic contribution to the development of the islands. That would be me.

§

As I mentioned earlier, it was not until fairly recent times that cruise lines made Grand Turk a port of call. It took a lot of planning and engineering to build docking facilities for those super-large ships.

When Noreen and I lived on Grand Turk, we would often see the project overseer, a man we called Carnival Jack, walking on the beach. One day we invited Jack in for a cup of coffee and engaged him in conversation about the vessel. Noreen asked, "Will we be able to see it from here?" Jack gave a wry smile and replied, "Oh yes, you'll see it."

Well, we later figured out what he was slyly referring to. When the ships made their way through the Passage to the dock, they would sail directly in front of our cottage, only about ¼ mile away. Being 17 stories high, the giant cruise-boat, as it was called in the Islands, could hardly be missed. In fact, it was quite visible even after it docked, some distance away.

§

You may wonder whatever happened to the Admiral's Arms hotel. Well, it was sold and became classrooms and dormitories for a worldwide educational program called The School for Field Studies. In the Islands, the specific focus was Marine Resource Studies. In fact, young

Embry spent a semester there earning college science credits toward the University of Montana's graduation requirements.

§

During our second stay there, Noreen and I were concerned that crime seemed to be accelerating, and getting closer.

André and Joan, our next-door neighbors were victims of a machete-wielding burglar one night. Somehow André, an attorney, was able to phone me during the incident. I grabbed a pistol and went to his aid, but the attacker ran off. Not before he put a slice in André.

More personal to me was the time that I woke in the morning to discover some things amiss—the door screen slit, my wallet moved, all the cash taken from it. That was disturbing because the wallet was on a table only three feet from where we slept. And Noreen and I didn't hear a sound.

The second break-in we experienced occurred when we were away, but it appears that the prowler may have been scared off before taking anything.

The third incident happened when we were in the States. It was not uncommon for thieves to break in houses of those residents who were not in the Islands year-round, and that was our situation. Upon our return, we discovered that a 10-horsepower motor from our boat had been carried a short distance and then dropped—it was probably too heavy for the burglars to easily carry.

So, things were changing for the Islands and for us— and not for the better. It was no longer like the '60s and '70s when there were few, if any, criminal issues to deal with. Back then the local police were on top of things and would visit the suspected bad guys for a talk or perhaps more. In 2005, my friend Sherlock Walkin remembered it in similar fashion: "The '80s was the thing—I loved it—the community was still closely knitted, everybody was like family. That has now changed."

We ended up selling the Grand Turk house in early 2008, months before the Islands were struck by Hurricane Ike, a major Category 5 storm, in September of that year. As a result of that windstorm, an estimated 80%-95% of the houses on Grand Turk were damaged, 20% of which were a total loss. There was also significant structural damage to roofs and buildings containing health services, resulting in the disruption of most medical assistance. The local pharmacy, police station, prison and local supply facilities were significantly damaged or destroyed. How did the house that we rebuilt fare? Well, it was not damaged other than the one piece of tin that was blown off the roof—probably because of the hurricane clips I custom-made and installed in the rafters.

Let me tell you more about those clips, which are meant to fasten the rafter to the wall plate. It seems that the contractor who was doing our renovation said he didn't see the need for installing them. That probably meant that he forgot to do so. So, I had to make them from a piece of aluminum and install them myself. What a job! But we did things right.

Fortunately, there were no hurricanes that directly hit the Islands during the 10 years that I flew there. There was one hurricane threat in the late 1960s that caused us to fly our planes up to Exuma in the Bahamas, about 300 miles away; but it turned out to be a false alarm. After we returned and bought the place in Grand Turk, we had a few scares, especially with Hurricane Frances in 2004, which passed 20 miles north of North Caicos.

Oh, yeah. There was one localized tornado that I witnessed on South Caicos. The huge wind that came up and I saw it start to spin the Cessna around on the ramp. Quickly, I ran to the aircraft, jumped in, started it and literally began to fly it in place to keep it from being blown away. It worked, and the tornadic gusts subsided after three or four minutes with the plane intact.

§

Meanwhile, back in Kentucky, we lived in the historic Clore House until about 1995 when we bought a townhouse condo in Prospect. While living in the condo, we planned and built a timber-frame house in Skylight, another town in Oldham County. It was a really neat place on 20 acres. An Amish group pre-cut the timbers, then assembled it after hiring a non-Amish trucker to haul it here.

Selling the townhouse was a unique real estate experience for us. The condo had a lot to offer. Located on Riding Ridge Road in Hunting Creek, it dead-ended on a golf course, with woods nearby. It was huge, with several bedrooms and 3,000 square feet of living space altogether. However, even under the experienced guidance of our go-to realtor, Mike Skelton, we couldn't get a decent offer.

After a while, Mike recommended a Dutch Auction. In front of the property, he installed a huge sign which declared that the price would be decreased $5,000 per week until the condo was sold. Of course, he started at a very high price. This action infuriated the neighbors, but the townhouse sold after three or four weeks, and at a very nice price.

§

The sale of Champion in 1998 meant that I was retired at the grand old age of 57. Although we were frugal and managed our money well, I was looking for another business to operate when disaster struck. We learned that Noreen had cancer.

Her first breast cancer diagnosis was in 2000, after which we started making a lot of trips to hospitals and doctor offices in Louisville and focusing on her treatment and recovery. She underwent surgery, then chemotherapy and radiation treatments, and the cancer went into remission. Then it reappeared in 2008. More treatments, more doctors and another remission followed.

During those tremendously difficult times, we were blessed with the birth of several grandchildren in the space of about four years. Siofra's daughter, Isabel May Nugent, was born on September 21, 2003; son Embry had two children: Embry IV, born on February 21, 2005, and Ennis Quinn, born on October 25, 2007. Siofra's first daughter, Tinsley Noreen Nugent, had been born on August 2, 1997.

§

In 2005, Rudy and I took a snorkeling, scuba diving and kayaking trip to Micronesia, an island region in the Western Pacific Ocean, between the Philippines and Indochina. This was a very enjoyable trip to a unique, magical place that allowed my brother and I to rediscover how much we honestly liked each other after these many years.

Growing up, I was probably the typical mean, but sometimes very protective, big brother. Our five-year age difference meant that we truly didn't have that much interaction in earlier years—due to the Army, college, my ten years in the Islands, his move to California and similar reasons. Although I went to his wedding in Geneva, and he came to the Islands a few times, we just didn't see a lot of each other for many years.

During his 1969 visit to the Islands, Rudy had dived at Grand Turk several times and enjoyed it immensely. Thirty-six years later, one of us brought up the subject of diving in the waters of Micronesia; so, we put our heads together, looked at each other's graying hair and said it's time to do it! We agreed to meet in Honolulu and then travel to Micronesia for three weeks.

My airplane itinerary took me from Louisville to Los Angeles, Honolulu, Guam, and the islands of Yap, Palau and Pohnpei, one of the four states in the Federated States of Micronesia. We spent one week at each of the last three locales. Our plan was to also travel to Kwajalein Island, but that part of the trip never materialized due to time constraints.

Among the sights we saw were huge clams with unbelievable iridescent coloring and giant manta rays that swooped over us during our dives off Yap. The marine and coral life were distinctly different from the Caribbean. In addition, we saw a lot of sunken ships from the World War II navies of the Allies and the Japanese.

While on Yap, the so-called Island of Stone Money, Rudy and I saw the huge money-stones that had been transported from an island that was hundreds of miles distant. What fascinating stories these stones could tell.

Someone on Grand Turk gave me the name of a woman working for a private non-profit organization on Pohnpei and said to look her up, and we did. Being two visitors from the United States, we were invited to a large party at which there was feast of food and drink. The locals prepared a large coconut shell by filling it with Kava root juice, and they gave it to me first since I was the oldest. Kava is a sedating or intoxicating drink consumed throughout the Pacific Island areas. Leaving out any incriminating details, suffice it to say that Rudy and I both proceeded to get a big buzz on it.

The native islanders whom we met in the Western Pacific were of a different type that those in the West Indies. They are both friendly, to be sure, but the Pacific Islanders were more culturally accepting than their counterparts in the Caribbean and West Indies. There was absolutely no racial animosity or cultural tension exhibited by anyone we saw.

As I indicated before, Rudy and I had a great time rediscovering each other during that trip. Now, I believe that we are closer than we have ever been.

§

The Church of God of Prophecy, which had many followers in the Islands, conducted its International Assembly in Louisville around 2006, and many members from the Turks and Caicos came up here for that convention. Noreen's sister, Ann Dempsey, contacted us and arranged for us to meet with some of the locals who travelled to Kentucky. We did a variety of things with them, including shopping and touring.

Interestingly, none of them had *ever* been to a zoo, and they were fascinated with the animals at the Louisville Zoo. Also, they were scared when we drove over the Kennedy Bridge to Southern Indiana—some had never been on a bridge before, and none on a span that high. There just weren't any zoos and bridges in the Turks and Caicos. The locals enjoyed their trip, and I hope that our hospitality provided a warm welcome.

§

After Noreen's cancer diagnosis, we decided to look for a house in Ireland, closer to her birthplace, so we could spend some quality time together. In 2005, we were lucky and found a cottage overlooking scenic hills and valleys at Corofin, only eight miles from her hometown of Ennis and her family in County Clare. The proximity allowed me to connect with her Irish relatives and to know them better. Noreen was a peaceful woman, never an anti-English Irishwoman, and she enjoyed her home isle immensely.

Anyway, the mostly-stone structure that we purchased was quite dilapidated and rundown, so we had to do a virtual rebuild of it. Sound familiar? The Irish were very strict on the remodeling of older structures, so we had to hire an architect. Although we couldn't add on to the existing residence, we were able to transform the permanent garage into extra living space.

Thus, we owned homes in Oldham County, Ireland and Grand Turk, spending most of our time in the latter.

§

In addition to her trips with me to Ireland, Noreen had travelled to China in 1995 with our good friend Phyllis Florman and really enjoyed it. The occasion was the United Nations Fourth World Congress on Women, and Hillary Clinton, then First Lady, was also there. Although Phyllis attended the famous speech focusing on women's' rights issues that Clinton delivered on Sept. 5, 1995, in a suburb of Beijing, Noreen chose to wander and explore the world's third most populous city.

Larry and Phyllis Florman and her brother-in-law, New York urban developer Tony Goldman, owned property in the South Beach neighborhood of Miami—specifically, the Park Central Hotel and the Tiffany Hotel, located in that city's celebrated Art Deco district. The Flormans introduced us to Tony in the mid-1980s, and we soon joined their partnership.

It seems that the Corps of Engineers had just acted to widen the beaches to about 600 feet in that area of Miami. Tony was a very savvy and successful real estate entrepreneur focusing on the restoration of older areas, and he believed that there would be a quick revival in the art deco hotel scene. He was correct. Noreen and I flew down there to inspect the properties, and I saw some investment potential. As it turned out, we partnered with him in three ventures: hotels, commercial buildings and a parking garage.

Tony built an attractive, landscaped parking facility which made a lot of profit each day since parking was so scarce in that area. In 1998, the Tiffany Hotel changed its name to The Hotel of South Beach, and it won numerous awards and accolades for its accommodations and service. Tony let it be known to all the travel photographers who were flocking to the South Beach revival area that they could stay at his hotel free of charge; then, he reaped the benefits of his kindness, by way of the free publicity that was generated. Eventually, Tony bought us out, but we did all right, and it was fun. We made some money on a decent return, and it gave us the excuse to travel down to South Beach a few times each year.

Another adventure that Noreen enjoyed was with our daughter. Siofra accompanied her mother on a horseback-riding trip to Portugal, which Noreen treated as quite a holiday. They were simply beautiful together.

§

Noreen and I had about five good years in our Irish cottage, until her cancer returned in 2010 for the final time. In fact, I was in Zimbabwe on a hunt when she called me to tell me that the disease had spread to her brain. I returned home immediately, or as fast as the airline schedules would allow.

Noreen Smythe Rucker was 67 years old and we had been married for 42 years when she finally succumbed to her cancer on Sunday, June 6, 2010 in Skylight, Kentucky. She was an accomplished horsewoman, farrier, gardener and a much-loved wife, mother and grandmother. Survivors besides me included her children, Embry and Siofra; four grandchildren, Tinsley, Isabel, Embry and Ennis; three brothers, Conor, Michael and Barry; four sisters, Ann, Olive, Maura and Maeve; many nieces, nephews and cousins; and countless friends. Services were held at St. Francis in the Fields Episcopal Church in Harrods Creek, and a reception followed at St. Francis.

But Noreen was so much more than that. My brother Rudy, who returned for the funeral and blogged about it, used the following words which rang so true:

"It's terrible to see a loved one's remains go into the ground, and to feel how heedlessly the greater world spins on. A death leaves a hole that's initially too big to take the measure of, too big and ragged for the bereaved to readily explore…Before and after the funeral, our assembled families ate endless meals, sitting on the front porch of my brother Embry's farmhouse. Talking, sometimes laughing, reminiscing, slowly beginning the process of grief.

"We had six grandchildren there in all—it was comforting to see the new shoots starting up, the saplings beside the fallen tree. I'm a mastodon compared to the grandchildren, an ice-age behemoth. The Reaper has moved down to my generation.

"Funerals are really for the survivors. The departed isn't there, at least not in any obvious way. But I'm always willing to entertain the long-shot thought that the deceased is on the scene in some form, perhaps as a butterfly, or as a puzzling light at night, or even as an invisible ectoplasm. But in any case, I doubt they're worried about the formalities. It's the people they would care about, the loved ones who are there.

"We'll miss you, dear Noreen. You were wonderful."

§

Noreen and I still had our adventures, even after her earthly passing. She desired that her ashes be spread in various places that were meaningful to her around the world. Arriving in Ireland to carry out her wishes, I discovered that the suitcase carrying her ashes had been lost. Protesting to the airline clerks, I moaned in dialect, "You've lost me wife's ashes, how can I now bury her?" The clerks were aghast and acted quickly to reunite me with her ashes so that I could accomplish my mission.

Who could have imagined that the exact same scenario would occur in Grand Turk upon my arrival to spread her ashes near the home that we shared in our later years. "Hey mon, no ashes," I yelled. Again, the locals acted quickly to remedy the situation. No doubt Noreen watched all this activity on her behalf with great amusement.

§

Shortly after Noreen's death, my good friend Richard Buddeke suggested that we go duck hunting. When I observed that it was not duck-hunting season, he replied, "The duck-hunting season is open in Argentina." So that's where he, Arlie Tucker and I went. After flying into Buenos Aires, we travelled to the middle of nowhere for a few days and shared a lot of laughs.

Previously in 1992, I had travelled for the first time to Argentina and Uruguay hunting birds, especially doves. These birds—by the millions—are considered agricultural pests in South America because they eat the crop seeds as fast as farmers can plant them. Poison was used ineffectively for years, before someone got the bright idea of marketing hunting trips for Americans who could shoot the pests right out of the sky.

Richard and I targeted a lot of different species there: some species of ducks were the same that we saw in Kentucky, others were indigenous to South America. Once, a flamingo flew overhead, and Richard pretended to prepare to shoot it, when the guides excitedly yelled, "No, Senor, No, Senor!"

§

My most recent visit to the Turks and Caicos was in August 2014, when I attended the funeral of my brother-in-law, Finbar F. Dempsey, who died at the age of 77 after a long illness. A Requiem Mass was held for him at the Holy Cross Roman Catholic Church on Grand Turk, and I was one of the elegists. Privately, we in the family always called Holy Cross "St. Ann's," because Finbar's wife Ann was a founder and a faithful member for many years.

Finbar Fiachra Dempsey was born in County Tipperary, Ireland, and came to the Islands in 1964 at the age of 27. He served as Chief Magistrate and legislative draftsman for the Turks & Caicos from 1965 to 1969. He was also the founder and principal of two law firms in the Islands.

Although he was basically a quiet man, Finbar loved to talk and have fun; he was a good friend to many. The St. Patrick's Day parties that he and Ann held were legendary, raucous events.

One memorable story that Finbar loved to relate concerned a trip he once made as Chief Magistrate to the small village of Bambara in Middle Caicos, when he was making the circuit. It seems that in each village, there was a small hut, called a Government Rest House, for use by the visiting officials.

On this particular trip, there was an outdoor privy that Finbar used. When finished, he did not see any toilet paper and looked around for some. Whereupon a hand came through a hole in the wall holding a roll of toilet paper! So much for any expectation of privacy.

As Chief Magistrate, Finbar was responsible for determining the punishment of various law breakers. Some of the punishments would not be doled out in today's world—in particular, "10 of the best."

For example, if a local young person was heard to curse or use bad language in public by saying G-D or M-F, they would be hauled before Finbar. If Finbar found them guilty, he may order Sgt. Manuel or Inspector Baker to give the lad 10 of the best, meaning 10 strokes with a stick or cane. This flogging was done in public, and it was a tremendous disgrace to the family of the miscreant. Typically, family pride kept the youth from re-offending. This was just one of the punishments that was accepted during those times.

In any event, my flying service enabled Finbar to be gone far less than the two weeks that it used to take him to make all his stops in the Islands. Ann was certainly grateful for that.

His wishes were that he be buried in the churchyard of Holy Cross; however, the church had never gotten around to having that site officially approved as a burial ground. His son Paul, who was also his law partner, went to the Governor, His Excellency Peter Beckingham, and said, "Look, we're burying my father in the churchyard in three days—you can either approve it or not." Needless to say, the Governor gave his official blessing.

§

Noreen's sister Maeve, younger by 18 years, visited Ann and Noreen frequently in the Islands; she came to enjoy life there so much that she sold Epicene, her business in the Ennis Town Centre, and her house in Ireland and moved to Grand Turk, buying a house and three rental apartments.

After breaking her leg and having an operation in 2014, she became ill with some kind of bone weakness and was transferred to University Hospital in Kingston,

Jamaica. Maeve died unexpectedly there at age 52. That was quite a shock.

Noreen's sister, Ann Dempsey, succumbed to cancer in a Providenciales hospital in August 2016, while I was working on these memoirs. She was 75. Her three children still live in the Islands. As I was not available to travel then, my daughter Siofra attended the funeral on September 2, 2016, as our representative; she was always close to the Dempseys. Ann, Finbar, Noreen and I were all great friends and had many good times together over the years.

§

Coincidentally, Noreen and I had earlier purchased our place in Skylight, Kentucky from Elizabeth "Lizzie" MacLean, who was the sister of the woman who would later become my second wife, Joanie MacLean. Their father was Angus MacLean, owner of the Wood-Mosaic Corporation in Louisville's Highland Park neighborhood, and son of the founder of that company. Founded in New York in 1883, Wood-Mosaic was a major business. It became a huge, diversified, hardwood-products company, employing over 800 people; at one time, it was the largest producer of fine face veneer in the United States.

Joanie and I first met when I was age 12, and we occasionally dated as adolescents. We even exchanged letters for a while after she went away to boarding school. Then we went our separate ways, as young adults often do. Eventually, we renewed our friendship when Joanie taught our children at St. Francis School in Goshen. Noreen came to know Joanie as a friend and liked her very much.

Joanie had three children from her prior marriage: One son, Stuart Ulferts, is an attorney who lives with his wife Kelli and family in Prospect; her daughter Elizabeth is married to Bill Reisert, President of Reisert Insurance Company; and, her son Erick Ulferts and his wife Julie and their family live in Portland, Oregon. So now, Joanie and I have a total of eleven grandchildren.

Sometime after Noreen's death, Joanie and I began seeing each other, and we dated for a year or so. Then on December 22, 2012, we married. Isn't it interesting how things turn out in life?

At that time, Joanie lived on Spring Drive, and I still lived in the house in Skylight. We decided that Oldham County was too far out; so, we sold both of those houses and moved to our current one at 2544 Glenmary Avenue. We bought it, then spent about six months putting the addition on it. This time, though, the contractors did all the work. Both of us love the house and its pool. And each other.

§

As far as flying goes, Larry Florman and I are co-owners of a yellow 1941 Piper Cub that we keep in a hangar at Bowman Field. At least once a month I will take it out and practice takeoffs and landings. The landings are more satisfying to me because they require a certain amount of skill and expertise. Sometimes I fly to Lee Bottom Flying Field, a privately-owned public airport with grass runways, located about six miles south of Hanover, Indiana. There is no minimum amount of flying time that is required for me to retain my pilot's license, but my aircraft must undergo an annual inspection.

Originally, Larry, Bill Renda, two others and I bought a Piper PA-18 Super Cub, a two-seater with a considerably stronger 150-horsepower engine. A well-renowned bush plane, it had considerably more room in the cabin than our current Cub, which is a pain to get into, especially for taller people such as me.

Piper Cubs are slow, but forgiving if something goes wrong—that's why they are good planes for young pilots to get experience. In addition to sightseeing in the air, I like to practice stalls. Like most pilots of small planes, I am always on the lookout for a field, road or other open space in order to make an emergency landing, if necessary. Although I don't carry a parachute, our Cub could probably glide to a decent enough landing. Joanie was only up with me one time, on a bouncy day. So, she is not crazy about going up with me again, but that's OK.

When all is said and done, I rank flying the DC-3 as my most challenging—and enjoyable—airborne experience. It was more complex and versatile, and you could land it slowly on short airstrips; plus, it could transport a huge load of cargo. I also enjoyed the small size, handling and versatility of the Cessna 180 and longer Cessna 185, with its large door in the rear. The Twin Bonanza was a lot of fun, too.

Once, I had the opportunity to fly a Boeing-Stearman biplane, which was a unique experience. There's nothing quite like flying with an open cockpit and having that huge radial engine immediately in front of you. This biplane was built in the United States and used as a military trainer aircraft during the 1930s and 1940s. Thousands of these surplus aircraft were sold on the civilian market after World War II. In the postwar years, they became popular as crop dusters, sports planes, and for aerobatic and wing-walking use in air shows. I'm not exactly sure which model I flew; despite all the variations, they were pretty much the same except for different engines.

Some time I'd like to fly a gyrocopter—they have interested me for a while. These planes look like small helicopters, but are actually powered by a propeller, not the large horizontal rotor blades.

One of the flyers that I have always admired is the highly-regarded, record-setting test pilot Chuck Yeager. It was my pleasure to meet General Yeager at an air show in Louisville. I had heard that he was a hunter, so I invited him to go dove hunting with me, but he politely declined my offer. Oh, well.

As for airlines in the Turks and Caicos, they come and they go, sometimes with a name change. Today, Caicos Express and InterCaribbean Airways, formerly Air Turks and Caicos, appear to be the two most active local flying services.

§

About a year after I came back to Louisville in 1977, my parents also returned from Virginia. Or at least my mother did. After many years of marriage, my parents separated in 1978 and divorced the following year. Father stayed in Virginia and mother remained in Louisville.

My parents passed away within several years of each other: Mother died on July 13, 1991 at the age of 74, and father died three years later at age 79.

Mother had a very rough last few years, complicated by her diabetes and strokes, the first of which occurred in 1989; then, they continued for the next two years. She had several caretakers who looked after her at home; however, at the time of her passing, she been residing in the Episcopal Church Home, a senior living facility.

Noreen and I were diligent in looking after her and caring for her. My brother and I survived her, along with her brother Conrad of Hanover, Germany, and five grandchildren. Her funeral took place at St. Francis in the Fields Episcopal Church in Harrods Creek, where she was buried. Mother wanted memorial gifts in her name to be directed to St. Francis in the Fields Scholarship Fund.

Father's health started declining about the same time and he ended up in a nursing home in Reston after several strokes. Oftentimes during his final years, I flew into Washington Dulles International Airport to visit him in Virginia. He died in Reston on August 1, 1994 at the age of 79. His obituary listed a friend, Priscilla Ames, who cared for him. He was buried at the Chestnut Grove Cemetery in Herndon, Virginia. Pop directed that memorial gifts be sent to St. Francis in the Fields Memorial Scholarship Fund; Friendly Instant Sympathetic Help (FISH) in Reston or Embry Rucker Shelter in Reston.

In 1987, it was a very nice honor for my father when the Fairfax County, Virginia Board of Supervisors renamed the local community shelter after him. He was a long-time Reston resident, minister and member of the Shelter Advisory Committee. Unfortunately, I was not able to be present for the official ceremony.

Operated by Reston Interfaith, the Embry Rucker Community Shelter is a 70-bed residential shelter that provides healthy, safe, emergency housing for families and single men and women. Staff there are dedicated to helping homeless clients and to facilitating their transition to stable housing. The Center is open 24 hours a day, 365 days a year and employs 20 full-time staff members. It also has several part-time staff and more than 400 volunteers dedicated to helping its residents get back on their feet. Quite an honor for our father.

Joanie and I attended the events surrounding Reston's 50th Anniversary Celebration at the Community Center in 2014. We took part in a private preview screening of a documentary film project titled *Another Way of Living—The Story of Reston, Virginia*. Surprisingly, my father had a significant role in this film and was on the screen many times. To tell you the truth, I was startled to see him on the big screen; it was a bit odd to see him larger than life ten years after his death. In fact, it was a very moving an emotional experience for me.

Mr. Robert Simon, the founder, who was 100 years old then, was himself a bit taken aback when I approached him and introduced myself as Embry Rucker—Junior. Then, he realized that he was not seeing a ghost, only his friend's son. Bob Simon passed away the following year. He was quite a genius of a man.

§

Joanie and I are fortunate to love the adventure that travel provides. We have travelled to France a few times, including a very moving trip to Normandy—I have always been interested in World War II, especially D-Day. After renting a car, we drove there from Paris. Luckily, we engaged an excellent guide, and just the three of us toured the area.

We were both pleased to take a wonderful month-long trip to Europe in autumn of 2016. Flying into Heathrow, I arranged to meet a taxi-driver friend of mine, Jim Clark, whom I have known for five years. Jim drives a Black Cab and is also a hunter. These drivers are licensed and must pass an extensive training course, memorizing over 20,000 locations and sights to see for visitors.

Then, we were off for six days in the Edinburgh, Scotland area, where I took aim at partridge and pheasant, before driving to Wales to hunt for same. Then back to London before moving on to Berlin for three nights—I hadn't been to the German capital for 50 years.

While in Berlin, we met Louisa, Uncle Conrad's granddaughter, and she showed us around the city. In fact, we were able to find the home in which my mother lived. That was remarkable. So was the trip we took to find my great-great-grandfather Hegel's grave and tombstone, also courtesy of Louisa's touring efforts.

Leaving Germany, Joanie and I travelled to Prague and the Czech Republic for three nights before returning to London. We dined for lunch at Rules, the oldest restaurant in London, established by Thomas Rule in 1798. Rules serves traditional food of England. It specializes in classic game cookery, oysters, pies and puddings. Rules is fortunate in owning an estate in the High Pennines—England's last wilderness—which supplies training in game management for the staff, exercises its own quality controls and determines how the game is treated. I ordered and dined on the woodcock—twice as large as the American variety. It was served complete with its long bill.

We also had lunch in London with Conrad's daughter Gabrielle, and we reminisced about our trip to Germany in 1953 when we played together as children. Gabrielle recalled that Rudy and I were not invited to Uncle Franz's wedding because "we were not well-enough behaved."

Gabrielle's son Edward, who currently lives in Dubai, is also interested in genealogy and has done much research into the Heron side of the family.

We concluded our journey with a concert at St. Martin in the Fields, the historic landmark Anglican Church at Trafalgar Square in the heart of London. That provided quite a contrast with music that I heard in the small churches of the villages in the Islands. I have always enjoyed Anglican choral music, and I continue to enjoy the music at St. Francis in the Fields Episcopal Church in Harrods Creek and at the Church of the Advent in the Highlands, when I am at home in Louisville.

§

In recent times, we have been attending the Church of the Advent on Baxter Avenue on a regular basis. The Rev. Dr. Tim Mitchell is the Rector. Fr. Tim is a native Louisvillian and graduate of St. X High School. Prior to the ministry, he was an investment advisor and banker. Interestingly, his brother is a Catholic Passionist priest—Fr. Joe Mitchell, who is President of the Passionist Earth and Spirit Center behind St. Agnes on Newburg Road.

Speaking of churches, I will end this narrative on an amusing note, recalling a trip that Joanie and I made to St. Thomas—the older Anglican Church on Grand Turk. (St. Mary's is the other one.) When we attended services there a few years ago, it happened to be Boy and Girl Scout Sunday. While making his remarks, the Rector noticed me sitting there, and he unexpectedly introduced me as "the Scout of the air," and the first pilot in the Islands and so forth. "Stand up, Embry," he ordered, and I did so. Afterward, as we were leaving church, a young boy approached me and shyly asked, "Cap'n Embry, may I have your autograph?"

Famous at last!

Photos

Captions are after the photos

1.

2.

3.

4.

5.

6.

7.

8.

9.

10.

11.

12.

H1.

H2.

F1.

F2.

F3.

F4.

F5.

F6.

F7.

F8.

F9.

F10.

F11.

Captions

THE ISLAND YEARS

1. Embry in a Cessna 185, Caicos Airways. 1968.
2. Cessna 180. 1968
3. The Seven Dwarfs carrying a Jeep.
4. Embry with crashed Cessna 180. Conch Bar, Middle Caicos. 1968.
5. Salina donkey. Salt Cay or South Caicos. 1969.
6. Embry and Noreen, near Reston, Virginia. 1969.
7. Grand Turk. Embry, Embry III, Noreen, Mom. 1973 .
8. Grand Turk Airport. Noreen, Siofra, Pop, Embry. 1973.
9. Grand Turk. Noreen, Embry III, Siofra, Embry. 1973.
10. Grand Turk, Embry III, Embry, Noreen. 1976.
11. House in South Caicos. Mom, Noreen. 1968.
12. In Haiti. Embry, D. Dumont and Philipe. 1975.

HUNTING IN AFRICA

H1. Ume River, Zimbabwe. Embry & 15' crocodile. 1994.
H2. Embry with Elephant tusks. Zimbabwe, 1990.

FAMILY PHOTOS

F1. Embry in front of Dressel Farmhouse. 1944
F2. Louisville. Embry, Rudy, and Mom. 1947.
F3. On *Karl Fisser* ship to Germany. Rudy and Embry. 1952.
F4. Grandma Lily von Bitter with Embry and Mom.1957.
F5. Portrait by Hal Taylor. Pop, Mom, me, and Rudy.
F6. Embry and Rudy on dive trip to Palau. 2006.
F7 Embry and Embry III. Noreen's funeral. 2010.
F8. Grandchildren Ennis and Embry IV. 2010.
F9. Tinsley, Siofra, Isabel. 2012.
F10. Embry and Joanie Maclean. 2012.
F11. Rudy and Embry at Pop's grave. 2006.

Notes

Family History

by Embry Rucker

> *"Your family history and pedigree is of interest*
> *to absolutely no one but yourself."*
> —Embry Cobb Rucker, Sr.

Let me briefly tell you some additional details about my mother and father and their ancestors, friends and relatives.

My mother's birth name was Marianne Alise Clara Margarete, but the United States Immigrant Inspector assigned to interview her upon her entry into the country in 1938 shortened it to just plain Marianne.

My mother's great-grandmother was Jewish, as was the wife of her grandfather Hans Rudolf von Bitter (1811-1880), which certainly was deadly problematic during the reign of Hitler and the Third Reich in the 1930s.

One of my mother's ancestors—Agnes Heron—was born in Dublin, Ireland and was a descendant of the Heron family, a household of well-known actors, actresses and singers with origins in Ennis, County Clare, Ireland. Coincidentally, Ennis was the birthplace of my late wife Noreen. Agnes later married a German named Wilhelm(?) Rahe, whom she met in Havana, Cuba. He owned a large sugar plantation there. One of their children ended up living in Ottawa, Canada. From my mother, I came into possession of the Rahes' silver tea set; also over the years, I was given silver items dated 1835 belonging to Tinsley W. Rucker and Howell and Mary Anne Cobb.

In addition to playing football at VMI, my father lettered on the swimming team and competed as a diver. One of his classmates was Richard M. "Dick" Kleberg, Jr., whose grandfather was the founder of the famous King Ranch in Texas, on which I have hunted.

In an exchange program of sorts, the daughter of a prominent industrialist named Fason had gone to Berlin to stay for a term with my mother's family—the von Bitters—while my mother travelled to the United States to stay with the Fason family. It so happened that Atlantic Steel Castings Company, the large iron and steel works business that my father originally worked for, was owned by the Fasons. So, there is circumstantial evidence that my parents initially met through some connection with the Fason family.

During World War II, Rudolf "Rudi" von Bitter, my mother's father, was a German banker, and sometimes he could smuggle a letter to us through his contacts in Switzerland, officially a neutral country. My grandfather had served as chief administrator or rittmeister in Hirschberg in the past. My Uncle Franz II (1912-1987), one of mother's older brothers, was a German tank commander who was captured on the Eastern Front and spent many years in a prisoner-of-war camp operated by the Russians; he was not released until 1950. Her youngest brother, Rudolf Immanuel von Bitter, nicknamed "Pitti," also was a tank commander and a senior lieutenant; he was killed at age 23 while fighting with the 8th Panzer-Regiment in the Ukraine in 1941. Uncle Pitti's grave marker is topped with a large Iron Cross, a traditional Prussian military decoration that was restored as a German decoration by Adolf Hitler in 1939. My uncle Conrad (1910-1992) also fought for Germany in World War II; he was captured by the Americans or British, held briefly and released.

It is interesting to note that Franz and Conrad were law school graduates who had not trained for combat until they were drafted into the German Army. Pitti, on the other hand, was a career soldier in the German Army—the Wehrmacht—not the Schutzstaffel (SS), the Nazi Party's military organization.

My father's oldest brother was Tinsley White Rucker IV (1909-1983)—named after their father—and his brother Cason was next oldest. My grandfather Tinsley W. Rucker III (1878-1941, d. in Philadelphia) (married to Elon Cason, 1878-1953, d. in Warrenton, Georgia) was the son of Tinsley W. Rucker, Jr. (1848-1926), a US Congressman from Georgia who had married Sarah Mildred Cobb (1854-1933), daughter of General Howell Cobb. By the way, there is a lot of confusion in official papers over the proper suffix to names in the family, but I believe the above to be most accurate. Of interest to fans of sports history, Tinsley, Jr.'s brother Jeptha Vining Harris Rucker was captain of the University of Georgia's first baseball team.

The Tinsley Rucker who started all this was Tinsley W. Rucker (1813-1863), who had served in the Georgia state legislature and was much admired in his hometown Athens. Genealogists can trace my Rucker lineage back about eight generations to Peter Rucker, probably a Flemish Huguenot from Antwerp, Belgium, home of the master harpsichord make, Andreas Ruckers. Peter settled in Virginia in the 1600s; he was the first of that name in North America. It is said that his ship foundered, he floated ashore on an empty rum barrel and the Ruckers have been there ever since!

Ruckersville, Virginia, located north of Charlottesville, began in the mid-1600s; Ruckersville, Georgia probably started as a result of a land grant after the Revolutionary War. My Rucker ancestors founded them both. Interestingly, I am a descendant of William Speer (1747-1830) of County Tyrone, Ireland, on my father's side, and I also have Irish ancestors on my mother's German side. Yes, sometimes genealogy is confusing.

The most recent Tinsley Rucker—Tinsley V—is my Uncle Cason's son. This cousin of mine is a graduate of the United States Military Academy at West Point who served in Vietnam and later became a medical doctor. He is now retired.

Let me digress for a minute to take you back to the 1800s and tell you about Howell Cobb, an ancestor of distinction.

Raised in Athens, Georgia, my great-great-grandfather, Thomas Howell Cobb (1815-1868), commonly called "Howell," was quite an American political figure. His uncle Howell Cobb, after whom he was named, had been a U.S. Congressman from 1807–1812, who then served as an officer in the War of 1812, and who was described as: "Cheerful, gregarious, and a talented jester addicted to talking, Cobb's fondness for fine food and wine was revealed by his physique. However, behind his jolly-fat man facade lay a shrewd and very ambitious politician."

As a Southern Democrat, great-great-grandfather Cobb followed in his father's footsteps and served five terms in the United States House of Representatives, including two years as Speaker of the House. Not only that, but he was elected as Governor of Georgia and appointed as Secretary of the Treasury by President James Buchanan. He is, however, probably best known as one of the founders of the Confederacy, having served as the President of the Provisional Confederate Congress, in which delegates created the Confederate States of America.

He also served as President of the Confederate Congress. I have an excellent depiction of him—taken from an old photograph or drawing—swearing in Jefferson Davis into office as President of the Confederacy in Montgomery, Alabama. Resigning to join the Confederate Army, Cobb became a Major General and fought in many battles. His reputation preceded him—in 1864, Union Major General William Tecumseh Sherman himself ordered his plantation burned to the ground during Sherman's march to the sea. This, after Sherman had been advised that Cobb was "one of the head devils of the Confederacy."

Howell Cobb and his wife Mary Ann Lamar Cobb (1818-1889) had 12 children, six of whom survived to adulthood. After the war, he returned to Georgia to practice law. He died of a heart attack while on vacation in New York City.

Howell's brother Thomas Reade Rootes Cobb (1823-1862) was a noted jurist whose home in Athens, Georgia has become an operational house museum. During the Civil War, he headed Cobb's Legion, also known as the Georgia Legion, a noted Confederate unit that engaged in many battles throughout that conflict. He was killed by a federal sharpshooter while leading his brigade during the Confederate rout of Union forces at the Battle of Fredericksburg. A famous *fictional* member of Cobb's Legion was Ashley Wilkes, a character in the novel and movie *Gone with the Wind*. When I was perhaps 10 years old, I remember my father poking me when that was mentioned in the movie, as the whole family watched it in our Crosley automobile at a Louisville drive-in movie theater!

Some years ago, I visited the T.R.R. Cobb House, a monument to the Southern way of life. Built in Athens in 1842, it was used for a variety of purposes in the 20th century, including as a fraternity house. Placed on the National register of Historic Places in 1975, it was eventually moved to Stone Mountain Park in 1985, to prevent its possible razing. When I visited it, it had been returned to Athens in 2005 and restored to the way it appeared in 1850. It was even painted pink, which the neighbors did not care for. The interior of the house contains actual furniture, paintings and silver from the 1800s. Also displayed was the actual Confederate battle flag from Cobb's Legion that was draped over his coffin.

Some years after that visit, I donated several antique items to the Cobb House. They included an ornate marble-topped table and a wash-stand and basin, both handed down through the family from my great-grandfather. I also gave them a vintage plateau, an oblong piece that sat on the top of a table, used for display of vases and other items. The curator was so excited about these items that he himself drove up from Georgia to take them back.

According to an application for membership in the Sons of the American Revolution submitted by Uncle Tinsley and approved in 1966, my great-great-great-great grandfather was William Speer of County Tyrone Ireland, who fought in the Revolution as an ensign in the North Carolina militia, on the staff of General Pickens. Having fought in several engagements, including the famous Battle of Cowpens, he was granted a tract of land in the Abbeville District of South Carolina for his services.

Having told you about some noted ancestors on my father's side of the family, let me now mention a person of great distinction from my mother's family—the philosopher Georg Wilhelm Friedrich Hegel (1770-1831), another great-great-great grandfather of mine.

Hegel was an important philosopher and German idealist about whom someone once said, "All of the great philosophical ideas of the past century... had their beginnings in Hegel." His works greatly interested Karl Marx (1818-1883), a philosopher widely regarded one of the most influential figures in human history due to his landmark theories regarding socialism, Marxism and Communism. I am fond of a popular quote linking these two great philosophers: "Marx stood Hegel on his head."

Hegel was my great-great-great-grandfather from my maternal grandmother's family. His renown lives on in the family: I have three female cousins who are named Hegel—whom I met for the first time at a family wedding in Germany.

According to my brother Rudy, our great-grandfather Carl Julius Rudolf von Bitter (1846-1914) was a judge in a court for administrative workers, and he lived on the top floor of a giant courthouse near the Berlin Zoo. His father Hans Rudolf von Bitter was President of the Prussian State bank; the family received the "von" in front of their name as a result of being ennobled in recognition of his work.

In 1945, the English occupation authorities asked my mother's father to be the Finance Minister of Lower Saxony; he declined, instead taking a position as Secretary of State, and later, chairman of the Central Bank of Lower Saxony. He died at the age of 77.

Background and Sources

by Harry J. Rothgerber

"With a memoir, you must be honest. You must be truthful." —Elie
Wiesel
"No! Never check an interesting fact."
—Howard Hughes

My first contact with Embry Rucker was in the summer of 2015 through Richard Buddeke, a mutual friend. The Buddeke family had retained me to assist their patriarch, Charles H. Buddeke, Jr., in recording his life's memories and stories. Charles, then 97 years old, had learned to fly at Bowman Field in the mid-1930s; in 1937, he piloted a Piper J-3 Cub during the first year of that airplane's production. It just so happened that Embry owns a 1941 Piper Cub that he keeps in a Bowman Field hangar; so, it was fortuitous that my client's son Richard would arrange for us to take a field trip there one afternoon.

Upon meeting Embry for the first time, I was impressed with the tall, good-looking, articulate man who obviously knew what he was talking about on the subject of flying small planes, especially in the bush. The three of us had an enjoyable few hours together, especially Mr. Buddeke, who would pass away quietly in his sleep two months later. Embry's hospitality was greatly appreciated by all.

Thus, I was pleased when Embry contacted me later that year about helping him revise and elaborate on the story he had drafted some 30 years ago, regarding his adventurous 10 years of flying in the West Indies. Meeting regularly with him over the next 22 months to uncover more memories of those unique and exciting times as he related them to me, I came to know Embry as a friend more than a client.

During my research of the Rucker family history and genealogy, I was struck by the descriptive similarities of the first Tinsley W. Rucker, as mentioned in his obituary, and his great-great-grandson Embry Cobb Rucker, Jr. Like his ancestor Tinsley, the Embry I have come to know is of high intelligence, skillful and successful, and a Christian in principle and practice.

In addition to the stories remembered and discussed by Embry, there are a wide variety of other invaluable primary sources that might be accessed by a family member wishing to learn more about the subjects found in these pages.

In Reston, Virginia in 1984, at the age of 70, Embry's father recorded memories of his youth in a 95-page comb-bound booklet titled *Being Raised*. He dedicated it with the following words: "This is written for my grandchildren, Georgia, Siofra, Rudolf, Embry and Isabel so that they can know that I, too, was a child once upon a time—and for all my other young friends." Quite descriptive, amusing and revealing, it proceeds from his birth through his years at Virginia Military Institute.

Franz von Bitter, Embry's mother's brother, typed a 10-page unbound reminiscence titled *A German Prisoner-of-War Sees Russia*, in which he reflects on the things he saw and learned during his four years in captivity in Russia during World War II. It is an interesting, first-person chronicle of Russian life at that time.

Embry also possesses a 50-page bound family history titled *The Heron Family*, written by Heron descendant W. L. Scott, a Canadian, containing Embry's mother's handwritten inscription, "For Embry and Noreen, Aug '68." This genealogical story begins with the birth of John Heron in Dublin in 1804—into a family that had previously lived in Ennis, County Clare—and concludes with the death of Mrs. R. W. Scott in 1905. Interestingly, Embry's second wife Joanie's family had roots in Ottawa, and she remembered that there were some Scotts in her lineage.

Embry himself penned a remembrance of an African hunting adventure with a comb-bound booklet called *Zambezi Valley 1990*. It provides an excellent account of his earliest big-game hunting expedition in Southern Africa.

An interesting reminiscence from his mother's side of the family was left by his "Tante" Gerda Margarethe Clothilde Kathe von Bitter (b.1919), first cousin to his mother, who wrote her 12-page, typed story in Toronto in 2004. It was generated by the 2003 marriage of Georgia Rucker, Embry's niece, to Courtney Lassiter. This fascinating Germanic family history concludes with Aunt Gerda saying, "I hope that I have been able to bring you a little closer to the outstanding 'personas' of your great-grandparents, who lived valiantly and bravely through the terrible times of Nazi Germany."

Other hardbound books of interest in Embry's personal library are: *Cobb and Cobbs—Early Virginians: A Report on One of America's First Colonial Families*, by John E. Cobb, Jr. (The Durant Publishing Company: Alexandria, Virginia, 1977); *Thomas R. R. Cobb: The Making of a Southern Nationalist*, by William B. Cash (Mercer University Press: Macon, Georgia, 1983); and, *The Rucker Family Genealogy: With Their Ancestors, Descendants and Connections*, by Sudie Rucker Wood (Old Dominion Press: Richmond, Virginia, 1932).

In his application to the Sons of the American Revolution, Embry's Uncle, Tinsley White Rucker IV, cited a couple of other historical reference books of interest, neither of which Embry has located. They are: Clarinda Pendleton Lamar's *The Life of Joseph Rucker Lamar* (The Knickerbocker Press: New Rochelle, New York, 1926) and *The Rucker Family History*.

Along the same lines, I reviewed an article titled "Master of a Typical Old-Georgia Plantation: Joseph Rucker, Sturdy, Honorable, Kind," by Katherine Pope Merritt, dated June 2, 1935 from an unknown newspaper. Joseph Rucker (1788-1864) was born in Ruckersville, Virginia, and gave that same name to the area in Georgia in which he settled in 1812. I highly recommend this 1500-word piece to students of the Rucker family.

As he mentions in the Preface, Embry interviewed at least 21 Islanders and ex-pats in sessions in which he tape-recorded their remarks. These were all later transcribed, and he still retains the transcriptions. The discussions ranged from the mundane aspects of everyday life in the Islands, to insightful comments about government, politics and leadership.

For further background on the Ashtons from Chapter 11, I suggest that you read *The Spirit of Villarosa: A Father's Extraordinary Adventures; A Son's Challenge* as told by Horace Dade Ashton and Marc Ashton with Libby J. Bywater (Minneapolis: Two Harbors Press, 2016). Embry's copy was inscribed by Marc "Butch" Ashton as follows: "For Embry, I hope this brings back many wonderful memories and hope you enjoy it. With best regards, March Ashton (Butch), May 12, 2016."

Embry's brother, the eminent, prolific, science-fiction and biography author Rudy Rucker, has written about his life in the book *Nested Scrolls: The Autobiography of Rudolf von Bitter Rucker* (TOR Books: New York, 2011). Embry appears in many noteworthy scenes throughout his brother's life. Rudy also writes at length about his family's history on the website Rudyrucker.com.

When I asked Embry to provide me with photos from his years in the Islands, I was disappointed that there were so few. He explained that there simply was no fast and convenient method for delivering a roll of film to a developer in those days. There was literally no place to develop film in the Islands other than a military base. You had to go to Miami or somewhere else in the States to do it. So, in the process of waiting for such an opportunity, rolls of film would often be misplaced, destroyed or exposed. Too bad.

There was one disappointment that I had in delving into Embry's genealogy. Being an avid baseball researcher and writer—Embry once attended a Louisville Bats minor league game as my guest—I had hoped that the great Baseball Hall of Famer Ty Cobb might be found in his family tree. No such luck. Embry reported that as a youth he asked his father, "Dad, are we related to Ty Cobb?" The response was, "I don't know, and no one in the family wants to admit it."

Notwithstanding that minor letdown, working with Embry Cobb Rucker, Jr. to discuss and record his many memories has been a singular pleasure for me. When I consider the foundation for Embry's vivid, factual and humorous stories, a quote from psychologist and writer Joyce Brothers comes to mind: "When you look at your life, the greatest happinesses are family happinesses." So it is with Embry.

Made in the USA
Lexington, KY
15 May 2018